Excel Applications for Accounting Principles

Gaylord N. Smith, MBA, CPA

Professor

Albion College — Albion, Michigan

THOMSON

SOUTH-WESTERN

Australia · Canada · Mexico · Singapore · Spain · United Kingdom · United States

THOMSON

SOUTH-WESTERN

Excel Applications for Accounting Principles, 2e

Gaylord N. Smith

Vice President/Editorial Director:
Jack W. Calhoun

Vice President/Editor-in-Chief:
George Werthman

Acquisitions Editor:
Julie Lindsay

Acting Developmental Editor:
Janice M. Hughes

Marketing Manager:
Keith Chassé

Production Editor:
Lora Arduser

Manufacturing Coordinator:
Doug Wilke

Compositor:
Cover to Cover Publishing, Inc.

Printer:
Thomson-West
Eagan, MN

Design Project Manager:
Stacy Jenkins Shirley

Cover Designer:
Craig Ramsdell/
Ramsdell Design

Cover Photo:
Courtesy of ©PhotoDisc

Library of Congress Control
Number: 2003105104

ISBN: 0-324-27027-5 (Book + CD)

ISBN: 0-324-20287-3 (Book only)

For more information
contact South-Western,
5191 Natorp Boulevard,
Mason, Ohio 45040.
Or you can visit our Internet site at:
http://www.swlearning.com

CONTENTS

MODEL-BUILDING PROBLEM CHECKLIST   173

MODEL-BUILDING PROBLEMS

MODEL-BUILDING CASES

PREFACE

Flexibility, power, and basic simplicity all combine to make a spreadsheet program called Excel very popular in today's business world. The most common uses of spreadsheet programs are for:

- budgeting and financial planning
- financial management and investment analysis
- preparation of financial statements, reports, and graphs
- performance of what-if analysis
- business documents such as invoices, customer statements, and expense reports

In addition to these uses, there are many other applications for spreadsheet programs: depreciation schedules, inventory control, tax planning and preparation, consolidations, statistical analysis, bookkeeping, and so forth.

The purpose of this workbook is to bring spreadsheet technology in to the accounting classroom. It is designed so that business students can learn about and use Excel while doing regular assignments in accounting. The workbook is generic in nature and may be used in conjunction with any standard textbook in accounting principles, financial accounting, or managerial accounting.

This workbook consists of over 50 sample problems, preprogrammed problems, model-building problems, and model-building cases. The Student Disk that accompanies this workbook contains the files you will need for Sample Problem A, the preprogrammed problems, and the model-building cases. Several additional problems can be found at the website http://smith.swlearning.com.

SAMPLE PROBLEMS

The workbook begins with four sample problems (A, B, C, and D) introducing students to the methodology for solving the three types of workbook problems. Students must complete the sample problems before attempting the corresponding workbook problems.

PREPROGRAMMED PROBLEMS

Problems are included for most of the conceptual areas covered in first year accounting courses. Students develop formulas and enter data to complete partially constructed spreadsheet models. After the basic solution is developed, students perform what-if analyses and interpret graphical information. All preprogrammed problems have optional sections (called ticklers) that stretch students' knowledge of Excel, including:

- redesigning and expanding the original model (Worksheet tickler)
- creating additional charts and printing them (Chart tickler)

MODEL-BUILDING PROBLEMS

Short problems from a wide variety of accounting topics are provided to give students experience in developing their own models. No computer files are provided for these problems. Two sets of data are included for each problem so students can build the model with one set and test their model with the other. An optional section of each problem challenges students to create a chart from the data.

CASES

Cases are distinguished from model-building problems in two ways: (1) cases utilize extensive data and require lengthy solutions and (2) the data for each case is collected in a spreadsheet file on the Student Disk. Like the model-building problems, cases include two sets of data and have an optional section with a chart assignment.

SEPARATE TUTORIAL AND REFERENCE BOOK

Some students have been introduced to Excel elsewhere, while other students are encountering this spreadsheet program for the first time. Students who have little or no experience using Excel are encouraged to buy a separate tutorial and reference book called *Excel Quick* by Gaylord N. Smith. It has been written specifically to accompany this workbook. Although it is not the purpose of this tutorial to teach extensive spreadsheet programming, it does cover all the basic commands thoroughly, including charts and business functions, and it introduces a few important frills.

Each of the five lessons *Excel Quick* takes about 30 minutes to complete.

Lesson 1— Covers entering text and numbers, editing entries, changing column widths, using toolbar buttons (italic, bold, align, underline, undo, sum, and borders), saving, and printing worksheets.

Lesson 2— Covers arithmetic calculations, number formats, designing formulas, using Excel functions, and displaying cell contents.

Lesson 3— Covers copying data, moving data, inserting and deleting new columns and rows, and centering data across columns.

Lesson 4— Covers global settings, special date formats, using the fill handle, establishing standard column widths, using accounting underlines, protecting cells and worksheets, naming cells and ranges, freezing columns and rows, using multiple worksheets at once, and adding artwork to worksheets.

Lesson 5— Covers creating charts, modifying and changing charts, enhancing charts with special features, using chart sheets, saving, and printing charts.

Appendix A— Built-in Excel functions for business applications.

Appendix B— Model-building hints.

Appendix C— Simple, real-world applications using Excel.

Although it is highly recommended, it is not required that *Excel Quick* be used with this workbook. At the instructor's option, *Excel Applications for Accounting Principles* and *Excel Quick* can be bundled together and sold at a discount (ISBN 0-324-28379-2).

WEBSITE

The website supporting *Excel Applications for Accounting Principles* can be found at http://smith. swlearning.com. Here you will find additional problem sets, links to real company financial statements in Excel format, and other valuable resources. This website also supports *Excel Quick* and contains several Excel business models that are useful for accounting, reporting, and investment analysis.

BENEFITS TO STUDENTS USING THIS WORKBOOK

The focus of this workbook is to facilitate spreadsheet use as an integral part of the accounting curriculum. Among the advantages to instructors and students of using this workbook are:

1. **Variety of what-if analyses.** Solutions to textbook problems generally result in a single answer. Solving textbook problems with a pencil and paper is generally quicker than typing everything into a spreadsheet model. So why waste time and energy just for the thrill of using a spreadsheet program? The answer lies in the spreadsheet's ability to perform what-if analysis. All the problems in this workbook utilize the tremendous what-if capabilities of spreadsheet programs to go beyond a single solution.

   After students develop the initial answer, they are asked a number of what-if questions. As a result, the spreadsheet models in the workbook are used not only to solve homework problems, they also reinforce the accounting concepts being taught in the classroom and they provide a demonstration of the instantaneous recalculative power of the spreadsheet program. As a result, the computer's capabilities are being *productively* used by students.

2. **Use of charts.** All problems in this workbook have optional chart assignments. Students are asked to interpret charts, create charts, print charts, and perform what-if charting. Charts are an increasingly important part of financial communications, and this workbook is unique in the special emphasis placed on it.

3. **Classroom tested tutorial.** The basic five-lesson tutorial in *Excel Quick* that introduces students to the world of Excel has been tested extensively in the classroom. Students are led through the Excel program in an efficient, step-by-step fashion. When students complete the tutorial, they will be prepared to work with existing models and to develop some reasonably sophisticated models of their own.

4. **Sound pedagogy.** In the design of the workbook, much attention has been given to supporting and enhancing the learning process. The learning process begins with a tutorial and sample problems that provide a sound foundation for completing the workbook problems.

The preprogrammed problems require students to use accounting concepts to solve problems with partially completed models. The model-building problems and the cases challenge students to use accounting concepts and their knowledge of Excel to design their own models.

Check figures are included for every problem. Appendices in *Excel Quick* provide useful information on functions for business and model-building hints. A particularly useful appendix provides several examples of Excel models that can be utilized in business.

INSTRUCTOR RESOURCES

Instructors adopting this workbook will be provided with a solution disk and solutions manual. The disk contains solutions to all parts of the preprogrammed problems and suggested designs for the model-building problems and cases. The manual provides all formulas and written answers required of the students, as well as all required printouts. The manual also contains suggestions on how to integrate the spreadsheet problems into the course, as well as other resource material. Instructors will also be provided with a password allowing them to obtain answers to the problems on the website http://smith.swlearning.com.

ACKNOWLEDGEMENTS

I wish to express my sincere appreciation to the many users of earlier editions of this workbook who have offered helpful suggestions. Colleagues in the teaching profession have been generous in contributing to the ongoing improvement of this workbook, and I thank you all.

I would like to acknowledge the excellent support I have received from the sales, editorial, and production staff at South-Western. Their commitment to the highest standards of quality and professionalism have made my association with them a pleasure.

This workbook represents an attempt to carefully combine the teaching of accounting with a well-planned, valuable exposure to Excel. I hope I have succeeded in my objective. Any comments, criticisms, or suggestions that you have regarding the workbook, its goals, and its organization are openly solicited and welcomed.

GAYLORD N. SMITH
Department of Economics and Management
Albion College, Albion, MI 49224
gsmith@albion.edu

INSTRUCTIONS FOR SAMPLE PROBLEMS

There are three sets of problems contained in this workbook: preprogrammed, model-building, and cases. With the preprogrammed problems, you will complete Excel files that have already been set up for you. You must finish the worksheet, experiment with the results, and then answer several questions to complete each assignment. The basic instructions for completing preprogrammed problems are found in Sample Problem A.

Each preprogrammed problem has two optional sections at the end—a Worksheet Tickler and a Chart Tickler. Solving the ticklers involves using spreadsheet commands to physically alter the appearance and/or components of the current model. In order to solve the Worksheet Ticklers, you will need some familiarity with spreadsheet modeling concepts and a basic understanding of spreadsheet commands. A sample Worksheet Tickler is shown in Sample Problem B. Sample Problem C serves as preparation for the Chart Ticklers.

With the model-building problems and the cases, you must develop models from start to finish. Model-building problems are generally not complex, but they take as long to complete as the preprogrammed problems because you have to design the whole worksheet model yourself. Cases are usually long, complicated problems and require substantial effort to complete. Sample Problem D contains a worked-out example of a model-building problem and includes hints for completing both the model-building problems and the cases.

As the following table illustrates, you must have some knowledge of Excel before attempting the sample problems. It is highly recommended that the book *Excel Quick* written by Gaylord Smith be used for this purpose.

| | Preparatory Materials | |
Workbook Problems	*Excel Quick* Lessons	Workbook Sample Problems
Preprogrammed	Lessons 1 and 2	Sample Problem A
Worksheet Tickler	Lessons 3 and 4	Sample Problem B
Chart Tickler	Lesson 5	Sample Problem C
Model-building and Cases	Lessons 1–4 (Lesson 5 optional)	Sample Problem D

1

Sample Problem A

SAMPLE PREPROGRAMMED PROBLEM

This sample problem is designed to acquaint you with the procedures used to solve the preprogrammed problems in this workbook. Each problem covers a different conceptual area in accounting. The problems are equivalent in length to standard accounting homework problems. Initially the problems may require a little more time than regular homework since you still may be somewhat unfamiliar with your spreadsheet program. Once you begin to feel more comfortable, your problem assignments should go quicker.

Before attempting Sample Problem A, you must have certain fundamental skills in Excel. You must be able to enter text and numbers, modify or delete entries, save and print files, use Excel to perform arithmetic calculations, use Excel functions, and design formulas using cell references. These skills are covered in Lessons 1 and 2 of *Excel Quick*.

The Student Disk provided with this workbook contains a spreadsheet file for each preprogrammed problem. Each file contains a worksheet that is generally divided into two sections—a Data Section and an Answer Section. The Data Section contains the quantitative information needed to solve the problem. The Answer Section provides the basic format for your solution.

The preprogrammed problems have the following parts: the problem statement, the problem requirements, a printout of the worksheet file, and the file itself, which is found on the Student Disk. The general procedures for solving the problems will be explained in the following paragraphs, using a sample problem. The sample problem appears in the boxed areas on the following pages.

First, read the problem statement shown in Illustration SP-1. The word SAMPLE in parentheses indicates the name of the file on the Student Disk for this problem. *Do not* open the file yet.

S1 ◆ FINANCIAL PROJECTIONS (SAMPLE)

PROBLEM DATA

Ecosys International is interested in estimating its net income for each of the next five months. It appears that January sales will be $10,000, and the company is hopeful that sales will increase by 2% per month. Selling expenses are roughly 60% of each month's sales, and general expenses average $1,900 each month.

Illustration SP-1   Sample Problem Statement

Next, read the first problem requirement shown in Illustration SP-2. This requirement states the basic aim of the problem and asks you to review the printout of the worksheet.

REQUIRED

1)   You have been asked by Ecosys International to provide net income projections for the next five months. Review the printout of the worksheet called SAMPLE. Note that the problem data have already been entered into the Data Section of the worksheet. Note also that the basic format for the solution has been set up in the Answer Section.

Illustration SP-2   Sample Problem Requirement 1

A printout of the worksheet is found at the end of each problem. The worksheet printout for the sample problem is shown in Illustration SP-3.

	A	B	C	D	E	F
2			*SAMPLE*			
3			*Sample Preprogrammed Problem*			
4						
5	Data Section					
6						
7		January sales		$10,000		
8		Sales growth rate		2%		
9		Selling expense ratio		60%		
10		General expenses		$1,900		
11						
12	Answer Section					
13						
14		Jan	Feb	Mar	Apr	May
15	Sales	FORMULA1	FORMULA2	$0	$0	$0
16	Expenses					
17	Selling expenses	FORMULA3	$0	$0	$0	$0
18	General expenses	FORMULA4	0	0	0	0
19	Total expenses	FORMULA5	$0	$0	$0	$0
20	Net income	FORMULA6	$0	$0	$0	$0
21						

Illustration SP-3   *Excel File for Sample Problem*

Notice the following features of the worksheet:

1. In the upper center of the worksheet, you will see the file name SAMPLE. You should always check the file name to see that you have opened the correct file from the Student Disk.
2. The work area of the worksheet is divided into two sections—the Data Section and the Answer Section.
3. The Answer Section contains several cells labeled FORMULA1, FORMULA2, etc. This indicates the cells in which you will be entering your formulas to solve the problem.

The next step is to write the formulas. Requirement 2, shown in Illustration SP-4, asks you to develop the necessary formulas. The formulas and comments on each are shown after the illustration. Use the information in the Data Section of the worksheet to develop these formulas. Wherever possible, formulas should incorporate cell addresses rather than specific values. The importance of this will be seen when you perform the what-if analysis in requirement 4. Write the formulas in the spaces provided in Illustration SP-4.

Illustration SP-4   *Sample Problem Requirement 2*

The formulas for the sample problems are below.

FORMULA1: **=D7**

Comment on Formula 1: January sales are given in cell D7 in the Data Section. This formula tells the program to use the value found in cell D7 as January sales in the Answer Section of the worksheet.

FORMULA2: **=D7*(1+D8) or =D7+D7*D8 or =B15*(1+D8)**

Comment on Formula 2: Any of these formulas will do. These formulas will calculate February sales as a 2% increase over January sales. March, April, and May sales are already preprogrammed in the worksheet. Note that you have expressed the growth rate as a cell address (D8). This allows you to change the growth rate simply by changing the number in cell D8 rather than by redoing the formula in cell C15. What-if analysis with different growth rates can be performed very quickly this way.

FORMULA3: **=D7*D9 or =B15*D9**

Comment on Formula 3: According to the problem statement, selling expenses are 60% of sales. Since January sales are already given in cell D7 (or cell B15) and the selling expense ratio is given in cell D9, you can simply multiply the two to compute total selling expenses for the month of January.

FORMULA4: **=D10**

Comment on Formula 4: General expenses are given in the Data Section in cell D10. This formula tells the program to take the value found in cell D10 and place it in cell B18.

FORMULA5: **=B17+B18** or **=SUM(B17:B18)**

Comment on Formula 5: Total expenses are the sum of the selling and general expenses. The =SUM function is frequently used in Excel models.

FORMULA6: **=B15-B19**

Comment on Formula 6: Net income is the difference between sales and total expenses.

After you have written the formulas in the workbook, the next requirement will ask you to start the spreadsheet program, open the proper worksheet file, and enter the required information. You are also asked to enter your name, save your solution, and print your completed file. Read requirement 3 shown in Illustration SP-5.

---

3) Start the spreadsheet program and open the file SAMPLE from the Student Disk. Enter the six formulas in the appropriate cells. Enter your name in cell A1. Save your solution as SAMPLE3. Print the worksheet. Also print your formulas. *Check figure: January net income (cell B20), $2,100*

Illustration SP-5   *Sample Problem Requirement 3*

Follow the steps listed below to complete this requirement.

1. Start the Excel program and insert the disk that accompanies your workbook in your computer's disk drive (usually drive A). Open the file SAMPLE from the Student Disk.
2. Check the file name printed in the center of the heading to make sure you have opened the correct file. If you have opened the wrong file, close the incorrect file and try again.
3. Notice that there are two sheet tabs at the bottom of the worksheet. One is called Worksheet and the other is called Chart. You will always begin your work on the Worksheet. Later you will use the Chart sheet. In fact in most cases, the chart on the Chart sheet will look odd until you have completed the worksheet.

4. Enter the six formulas required to complete the worksheet. All the cells that already have numbers or zeros in them have been preprogrammed with the correct formulas. To enter the required formulas, move to the appropriate cells and type the formulas you wrote in requirement 2. For example, to enter FORMULA1, move to cell B15 and type **=D7**. As you type these formulas, you will see the rest of the worksheet fill in with numbers. When you have entered these formulas, the result should be as shown in Illustration SP-6.

6

	A	B	C	D	E	F
1	Student Name					
2			SAMPLE			
3			Sample Preprogrammed Problem			
4						
5	Data Section					
6						
7		January sales		$10,000		
8		Sales growth rate		2%		
9		Selling expense ratio		60%		
10		General expenses		$1,900		
11						
12	Answer Section					
13						
14		Jan	Feb	Mar	Apr	May
15	Sales	$10,000	$10,200	$10,404	$10,612	$10,824
16	Expenses					
17	Selling expenses	$6,000	$6,120	$6,242	$6,367	$6,495
18	General expenses	1,900	1,900	1,900	1,900	1,900
19	Total expenses	$7,900	$8,020	$8,142	$8,267	$8,395
20	Net income	$2,100	$2,180	$2,262	$2,345	$2,430
21						

Illustration SP-6   *Screen Display of Completed Model*

5.   Check figures are provided for all preprogrammed problems. The check figure for SAMPLE, requirement 3, is January net income, $2,100. Verify that it agrees with your worksheet.
6.   Move to cell A1 and enter your name.
7.   Save your completed file now under the file name SAMPLE3. To do this, select the File Save As command and enter the file name **SAMPLE3**. Make sure the drive is properly specified for your Student Disk (usually drive A) and then click OK.

WARNING: You may receive the following message:

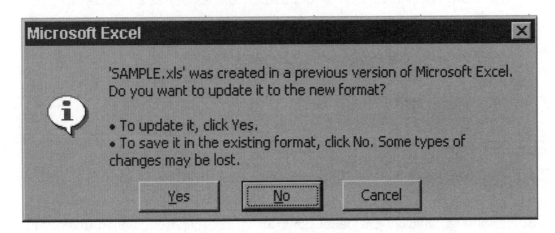

7

If you wish to update this file for the version of Excel you are using, click "Yes." Otherwise, click "No." Nothing is lost under a newer version of Excel. All workbook files work equally well under all formats.

Occasionally you may see the following warning:

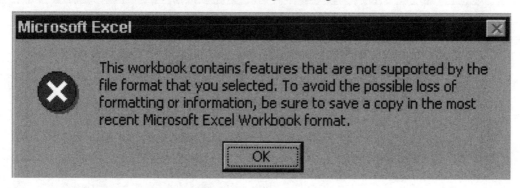

Just click OK. Everything works.

A word about using the file name SAMPLE3. If you had saved the file as SAMPLE instead of SAMPLE3, you would have wiped out the original file. This would cause no huge problem, but if you had really messed up SAMPLE3, you could at least go back to the original SAMPLE and start over.

If you run out of room on your Student Disk to save additional files, you may wish to delete some unneeded files from the disk. For example, the SAMPLE files may be deleted after all of the sample problems are done. Also, each original preprogrammed problem file can be deleted after the initial solution file has been developed, debugged, and saved.

8. To print the file, you will use the normal print commands. Long files will print on appropriately spaced pages without any special instructions from you. Also, worksheets will print with row and column headers showing.

9. Printing your formulas is a simple three-step process.
    (1) Use the mouse to highlight a rectangular area that includes all your formulas. On SAMPLE 3, select the range B15 to C20. This range includes all six formulas plus a few extra cells.
    (2) Hold down the **CTRL** key and press the **tilde** (~) key. This exposes all the formulas in the cells.
    (3) Select the File print command, choose the Selection button under "Print what," and click OK. The printout of your formulas should appear as shown below.

	B	C
15	=D7	=B15*(1+D8)
16		
17	=B15*D9	=IF((B17=0),0,(C15*D9))
18	=D10	=IF((B18=0),0,D10)
19	=B17+B18	=IF((B19=0),0,(C17+C18))
20	=B15-B19	=IF((B19=0),0,(C15-C19))

Some formula printouts are better done using landscape orientation and/or fit-to-1 page scaling. Where applicable, you will be instructed to select these options.

The next section of each problem is called "What-If Analysis." Illustration SP-7 shows the what-if analysis stated in requirement 4 of the sample problem.

WHAT-IF-ANALYSIS

4) The two options appearing below are being considered to improve the company's monthly net income over the next five months. Evaluate the effect on net income for each of these options. Consider each case separately. After evaluating each suggestion, enter the monthly projected net income in the spaces provided below. Assume that both options can be accomplished immediately.

OPTION A: Increase the sales commission rate. This means that sales personnel will receive higher commissions when sales are made. This will increase the selling expense ratio to 70%, but it is also expected to increase the sales growth rate from 2 to 5% per month.

OPTION B: Take some salespeople off commissions and put them on a straight salary. As a result of this, it is expected that the selling expense ratio will drop to 50%, but general expenses will increase from $1,900 to $2,900 per month. Also, the sales growth rate will drop to 1% per month.

PROJECTED MONTHLY NET INCOME

	January	February	March	April	May
OPTION A	_____	_____	_____	_____	_____
OPTION B	_____	_____	_____	_____	_____

Recommendation:

Illustration SP-7   *Sample What-If analysis Requirement*

This what-if question asks you to assess the effect of changes to the original data. The ease with which you will be able to manipulate the problem data and assess the impact on the problem results is an important part of understanding the power and flexibility of spreadsheet programs. This is the main reason for setting up a separate Data Section for most problems and for structuring the formulas using cell references wherever possible.

To explore Option A, move to cell D8 and change it to **.05**. Then move to cell D9 and enter **.7**. The worksheet should appear as shown in Illustration SP-8.

	A	B	C	D	E	F
1	Student Name					
2			*SAMPLE*			
3			*Sample Preprogrammed Problem*			
4						
5	Data Section					
6						
7		January sales		$10,000		
8		Sales growth rate		5%		
9		Selling expense ratio		70%		
10		General expenses		$1,900		
11						
12	Answer Section					
13						
14		Jan	Feb	Mar	Apr	May
15	Sales	$10,000	$10,500	$11,025	$11,576	$12,155
16	Expenses					
17	Selling expenses	$7,000	$7,350	$7,718	$8,103	$8,509
18	General expenses	1,900	1,900	1,900	1,900	1,900
19	Total expenses	$8,900	$9,250	$9,618	$10,003	$10,409
20	Net income	$1,100	$1,250	$1,408	$1,573	$1,747
21						

Illustration SP-8   *Screen Display for Option A*

Note that if the growth rate and selling expense ratio had not been separately listed in the Data Section, you would have had to change several formulas to analyze Option A. Instead, all you had to do was change two numbers!

In the space provided in Illustration SP-7, write the monthly net incomes. Refer to your printout from requirement 3 to see if the results are better or worse than the original projection.

To assess Option B, move to cell D8 and change it to **.01**. Move to cell D9 and change it to **.5**. Finally, move to cell D10 and change it to **2900**. Write your answers in the space provided in Illustration SP-7. The results of Option B should appear as shown in Illustration SP-9.

	A	B	C	D	E	F
1	Student Name					
2			SAMPLE			
3			Sample Preprogrammed Problem			
4						
5	Data Section					
6						
7		January sales		$10,000		
8		Sales growth rate		1%		
9		Selling expense ratio		50%		
10		General expenses		$2,900		
11						
12	Answer Section					
13						
14		Jan	Feb	Mar	Apr	May
15	Sales	$10,000	$10,100	$10,201	$10,303	$10,406
16	Expenses					
17	Selling expenses	$5,000	$5,050	$5,101	$5,152	$5,203
18	General expenses	2,900	2,900	2,900	2,900	2,900
19	Total expenses	$7,900	$7,950	$8,001	$8,052	$8,103
20	Net income	$2,100	$2,150	$2,201	$2,252	$2,303
21						

Illustration SP-9   *Screen Display for Option B*

What is your recommendation regarding these two options? Write your answer in the space provided in Illustration SP-7. Your written answer would be roughly as follows: Given the worksheet results, it seems clear that neither of these two options improves the company's net income projection for the next five months, and both should be rejected.

Your instructor may require you to print the file for each of the what-if scenarios. You will use normal print commands to do this.

The final requirement of each problem is a section entitled "Graphical Analysis." Requirement 5 of the sample preprogrammed problem is shown in Illustration SP-10. To begin solving this requirement, you are asked to reset the Data Section to its initial values. To do this, set cell D8 to **.02**, cell D9 to **.6**, and cell D10 to **1900**. Then click the Chart sheet tab. Immediately you will be moved to the second sheet in the SAMPLE3 file and will see the line chart shown in Illustration SP-11.

CHART ANALYSIS

5) Reset the Data Section to its initial values and click the Chart sheet tab. A chart appears on the screen indicating the relationship between sales and total expenses over the five-month period. The gap between sales and total expenses is net income.

A common interest of managers is a company's break-even point. This is the sales volume at which a company's dollar sales are equal to its total expenses. At the break-even point, net income is zero. Only when a company operates above the break-even point will it have profits. Use the chart to find Ecosys International's break-even point and enter the amount below.

Break-even sales $_____

HINT: Find a January sales level (cell D7 on the Worksheet) which causes the two lines to cross. The point at which the two lines cross is the break-even point.

When the assignment is complete, close the file without saving it again.

Illustration SP-10   Sample Chart Analysis Requirement

Notice that the sales line is above the total expense line. Thus, with a January sales volume of $10,000, Ecosys International will earn a positive net income each month because sales are greater than total expenses.

Click the Worksheet sheet tab to return to the worksheet and enter **8000** in cell D7. Click the Chart sheet tab again. Notice that the sales and total expenses lines are closer together, but they do not cross. Try different values in cell D7 on the worksheet and check the chart after each try until you get the lines to cross.

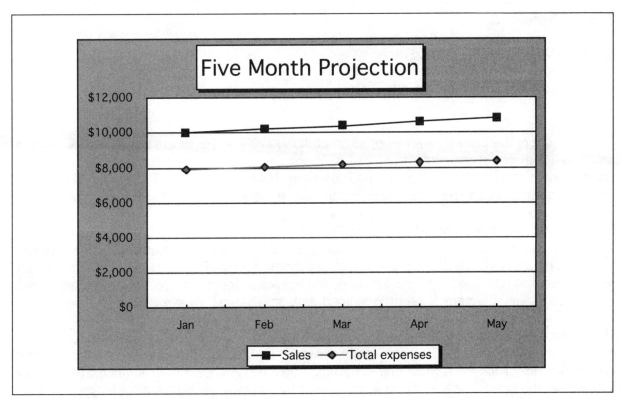

Illustration SP-11   *Line Chart*

A January sales level between $4,400 and $4,750 will result in the sales and total expenses lines crossing on the screen. As you read the chart, you will see that the break-even point is sales of $4,750. At this level of sales, net income is zero. You should now write this answer in the space provided in Illustration SP-10.

You have now completed the sample preprogrammed problem. Your final instruction is to close the SAMPLE3 file without saving it again. Do that now.

You may erase the file SAMPLE from your Student Disk to make more room for other preprogrammed problem solution files. **You must keep the file SAMPLE3 on your Student Disk because it is needed for the sample tickler problems that follow.**

Sampie Problem B

SAMPLE WORKSHEET TICKLER

The final part of the preprogrammed problems are the ticklers. These are optional sections that differ from the rest of the problem in that their solutions involve altering the worksheet itself. There are two ticklers for the problems—a Worksheet Tickler and a Chart Tickler. The Worksheet Tickler is covered in Sample Problem B and the Chart Tickler is covered in Sample Problem C.

Before attempting the sample Worksheet Tickler, you must have certain skills in Excel. You should be able to copy and move data, insert and delete rows and columns, change column widths, use a wide variety of Toolbar buttons, use the fill handle, freeze panes, and add artwork spreadsheet models. These skills are covered in Lessons 3 and 4 of *Excel Quick*. You also need to have completed the sample preprogrammed problem (Sample Problem A).

The purpose of Worksheet Ticklers is to demonstrate to you that the workbook files are not carved in stone and that they may be readily adapted to different facts and circumstances. The Worksheet Tickler for the sample preprogrammed problem is shown in Illustration SP-12. After you worked through Sample Problem A, you saved your answer as file SAMPLE3. Open that file now.

TICKLERS (OPTIONAL)

Worksheet. Late in December, Ecosys International had to obtain a bank loan to pay some business debts. The interest expense for this loan will amount to $300 per month. Alter the SAMPLE3 worksheet to include interest expense as an additional input item in the Data Section and also include the interest as an additional expense in the Answer Section (put it under General expenses). Put your name in Cell A1. Use the Print Preview command (File menu) to make sure that the worksheet will print neatly on one page, then print the worksheet. Save the completed file as SAMPLET.

Illustration SP-12   *Sample Problem Worksheet Tickler*

After opening the file, you must unprotect it. To do this, select the Protection command (Tools menu), and choose the Unprotect Sheet option.

The Worksheet Tickler asks you to insert an additional expense into the model. To add the additional expense to the Data Section, move to row 11 and insert a new row (Rows command [Insert menu]). In cell B11, enter **Interest expense**. Then enter **300** in cell D11.

Notice that the $300 in cell D11 is already properly formatted and unprotected. When you use the Insert Rows command, new rows will have the same formatting as the row just above the insertion.

To alter the Answer Section, use the following steps:

1. Move to row 20 (old row 19) and insert a new row (Insert Rows command) under General expenses.
2. Once again the Insert command has copied styles to the new row. The underlines in row 19 have been copied to row 20. To get rid of the underlines in row 19, select the range B19 to F19. Then click the Borders button and choose the border style that has no borders (upper left corner option).

Borders

3. In cell A20, press the SPACEBAR five times and enter **Interest expense**.
4. In cell B20, enter the formula **=$D11** (or type = and point to D11 and press **F4** [ABS] three times). The $ is needed for step 5 since you want the D in D11 to be absolute. Again, note that the cell is already properly formatted.
5. Copy the formula in cell B20 to cells C20 through F20. To do this, select cell B20 and click the Copy button. Then select the range C20 to F20 and click the Paste button. Notice that the gray shading in cell B20 is also copied. This can be cleaned up later.

Copy   Paste

6. Modify the total expenses formula for January using either of the following formulas:

   B21:=B18+B19+B20 or **@SUM(B18:B20)**

7. Copy the total expense formula for January to the other cells in that row using the Copy and Paste buttons.
8. If you wish to remove the gray shading in the copied cells, first select the range of cells from C20 to F21. Then choose the Cells command (Format menu) and click the Patterns tab. Pick the No Color option and click OK.

9. If you wish to change the bold, blue font in the copied cells, select the range of cells from C20 to F21. Then choose the Cells command (Format menu) and click the Font tab. Pick the color Black and Font Style Regular. Then click OK.
10. Type your name in cell A1.

When you are done, the worksheet should appear as shown in Illustration SP-13.

	A	B	C	D	E	F
1	Student Name					
2			SAMPLE			
3			Sample Preprogrammed Problem			
4						
5	Data Section					
6						
7		January sales		$10,000		
8		Sales growth rate		2%		
9		Selling expense ratio		60%		
10		General expenses		$1,900		
11		Interest expense		$300		
12						
13	Answer Section					
14						
15		Jan	Feb	Mar	Apr	May
16	Sales	$10,000	$10,200	$10,404	$10,612	$10,824
17	Expenses					
18	Selling expenses	$6,000	$6,120	$6,242	$6,367	$6,495
19	General expenses	1,900	1,900	1,900	1,900	1,900
20	Interest espense	300	300	300	300	300
21	Total expenses	$8,200	$8,320	$8,442	$8,567	$8,695
22	Net income	$1,800	$1,880	$1,962	$2,045	$2,130
23						

Illustration SP-13   Completed Worksheet Tickler

To reprotect your altered worksheet, select the Protection command (Tools menu) and choose the Protect Sheet option.

To avoid wasting paper on an improperly spaced printout, you should preview the printout before printing it. Select the Print Preview command (File menu) to view your file now. With this particular Worksheet Tickler, the modifications do not significantly alter the page layout so you will see that the revised model will print neatly on one page. If you do encounter a case where the modified printout appears to be sloppy (e.g., stray columns of numbers, etc.), you can clean it up using forced page breaks.

Print the worksheet now using normal print commands.

Save your modified masterpiece using the file name SAMPLET (File Save As).

After your instructor has reviewed your work, you may delete SAMPLET to create more room on your Student Disk for future homework files. **You must keep SAMPLE3 on your disk for the Chart Tickler (Sample Problem C).**

Sample Problem C

SAMPLE CHART TICKLER

The purpose of Chart Ticklers is to introduce the various charting options available in the spreadsheet program. Before attempting the sample Chart Tickler, you must have certain skills in Excel. You should be able to create and modify a basic chart, move it, resize it, print it, and save it. These skills are covered in Lesson 5 of *Excel Quick*. You also need to have completed the sample preprogrammed problem (Sample Problem A).

The Chart Tickler for the sample preprogrammed problem is shown in Illustration SP-14.

Chart. Using the SAMPLE3 file, prepare a chart that shows what happened to May's sales revenue (i.e., the percentage spent for selling expenses, general expenses, and the amount left over for net income). Complete the Chart Tickler Data Table and use it as a basis for preparing the chart. Put your name somewhere on the chart. Save the modified file as SAMPLE3 again. Print the chart.

Illustration SP-14   *Sample Problem Chart Tickler*

To begin the tickler, open SAMPLE3 from your Student Disk and do the following:

1. After opening the file, click the Chart sheet tab and move to row 42. If the problem you are working on uses a Chart Tickler Data Table, this is where it will always be. To complete this table, the range E44 to E46 needs to be filled in based on data from the worksheet. Generally you can enter either formulas or the values themselves. You are encouraged to enter formulas wherever possible since this will maximize your chart's what-if potential.
2. Click in cell E44. Before working on this sheet, you must unprotect it. To do this, select the Protection command (Tools menu), and select the Unprotect Sheet option.
3. Now that the sheet is unprotected, in cell E44 press the = (equal sign), click the Worksheet tab, select cell F17, and press ENTER. This places the formula =Worksheet!F17 in cell E44 and the value $6,495 should appear.
    Next, repeat this process to enter **=Worksheet!F18** in cell E45 and **=Worksheet!F20** in cell E46. Your completed Chart Tickler Data Table should appear as shown in Illustration SP-15.

	A	B	C	D	E	F
39						
40						
41						
42				Chart Tickler		
43				Data Table		
44				Selling	$6,495	
45				General	1,900	
46				Net income	$2,430	
47						

Illustration SP-15   *Sample Chart Tickler Data Table*

4. Select the range D44 to E46 and click the Chart Wizard button.
5. Complete the following four steps. Step 1—Your first decision is what type of chart you want. Line charts are recommended for showing behaviors over a time period, bar charts are good for comparing different items at the same point in time, and pie charts are used to show the relative proportion of elements that make up a whole. A pie chart is what you want in this tickler. Select the pie chart and pick the sub-type showing a 3-D Pie chart (middle option, top row). Then click Next. Step 2—Click Next. Step 3—For the title, enter **Distribution of May Sales** in the title box. Then click the Data Labels tab. Data Labels show certain kinds of data right on the face of the chart. Select the Data Labels to "Show percent," and click Next. Step 4—Click Finish.
6. There are a number of ways to put your name on the chart. The three most convenient ways to do this are (1) add your name to the chart title, (2) use your name as an X-axis or Y-axis title, or (3) use a text box from the Drawing Toolbar. You can also use WordArt from the Drawing Toolbar. Option 2 cannot be used on a pie chart, but the other two options will be demonstrated here.

   Select the title in the chart now. Then place the blinking insertion line right after the small "s" in Sales and press ENTER. This expands the title to a second line. Type in your name. You can put it in a smaller font if you want. Click elsewhere when done.

   To use a text box, activate the Drawing Toolbar by clicking the Drawing button. Then click the Text Box button and draw a box somewhere on the chart. Type your name inside the box and use whatever formatting commands you feel are appropriate. Click elsewhere when done.
7. Illustration SP-16 is how your chart might look. Save the file again as SAMPLE3 (use File Save).
8. Select the chart and print it out using normal print commands.

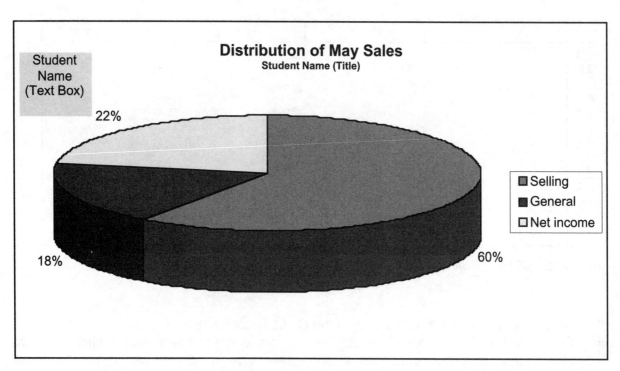

Distribution of May Sales
Student Name (Title)

Student Name (Text Box)

22%

18%

60%

■ Selling
■ General
□ Net income

Illustration SP-16 *Completed Chart Tickler*

Sample Problem D

SAMPLE MODEL-BUILDING PROBLEM

Model-building problems require you to design spreadsheet models from start to finish. Nothing has been done for you. Completing the model-building problems will require a thorough knowledge of basic Excel skills. Lessons 1 through 5 of *Excel Quick* should serve you well. In addition to the lessons, the tutorial provides three helpful appendices designed to assist in the model-building task. Appendix A covers built-in Excel functions useful for business models. Appendix B provides basic suggestions for developing spreadsheet models. Appendix C describes and shows several real-world applications of Excel.

The model-building problems contain two sets of input plus an optional chart section. The first set of input is for you to use in designing your model. The second set will be used by your instructor to test your model to see if it performs the proper computations. Your instructor should not have to change anything in your model except the input data. Thus, you must be very careful in structuring your model.

You have been provided with both sets of data so that you can:

- specifically identify which variables in the problem will change and which ones won't
- double-check your model to see that it functions properly with different inputs

The purpose of this sample problem is to show you how to approach the model-building problems in this workbook. To accomplish this, you will work through the sample model-building problem that appears in Illustration SP-17. Read the problem now.

ORIGINAL DATA SOLUTION

Before turning on the computer, some attempt should be made to lay out the structure of your answer on paper. Careful planning on paper can eliminate hours of wasted time on the computer. Fortunately, spreadsheet programs are forgiving enough that most refinements to a preliminary plan can be done "on the fly" while working at the computer.

M# TRIAL BALANCE

The general ledger of Thistle Consulting shows the following account balances at May 31:

Cash	$ 8,217.10
Accounts receivable	94,062.28
Accounts payable	21,665.38
Chris McKeon, capital	80,614.00

Chris Mckeon has asked you to develop a worksheet (file name BAL) that will present these numbers in a balance sheet format. Use the data above as input for your model.

Review the Model-Building Checklist on page 173 to ensure that your worksheet is complete. Print the file when done. *Check figure: Asset total, $102,279.38.*

To test your model, use the following balances at June 30:

Cash	$31,484.20
Accounts receivable	65,415.51
Accounts payable	10,544.48
Chris McKeon, capital	86,355.23

Print the file again. *Check figure: Asset total, $96,899.71.*

CHART (optional)

Prepare a chart that compares the individual asset balances at the end of May with the balances at the end of June. Print the chart when done.

Illustration SP-17   *Sample Model-Building Problem*

This model-building problem requires you to develop a spreadsheet model that is a balance sheet. Assuming you have had beginning accounting, you can probably visualize the answer format rather quickly. You might sketch out the following on paper to get you started.

Cash	$ 8,217.10	A/P	$21,665.38
A/R	94,062.28	Capital	80,614.00
	$ SUM		$ SUM

This is roughly what the answer will look like. The next major question to resolve is whether or not to use a Data Section for all of the changeable input values required to complete the model. A Data Section should always be given strong consideration since it helps highlight the numerical assumptions of the model, and it facilitates performing what-if analysis.

This decision relies on your judgment. As mentioned in Appendix B of *Excel Quick*, a direct-entry model is more appropriate than one using a Data Section in those cases where formulas do not have to be revised to accommodate the introduction of new data. In this balance sheet model, there are only two formulas (the sums at the bottom of each column), and they do not need to be rewritten as new data (account balances) are entered. Therefore, a direct-entry model (i.e., no Data section) is better for this particular model.

Now let's begin work on the computer. Start the spreadsheet program and, in the appropriate drive, insert the Student Disk or some other formatted disk.

You should enter your name and the file name somewhere at the top of the worksheet. As a suggestion, enter your name in cell A1. Enter the file name given to you in the problem in cell A2. The file name given for this problem is BAL. Do this now.

You will learn very quickly that making and correcting mistakes is a frequent occurrence when building models. Thus, in the instructions that follow, you will be purposely led into making a couple of mistakes and then shown how to correct them. Also, the Undo button can be very helpful for many types of errors. Turn to page 173 and review the Model-Building Checklist for some design suggestions.

Based on your initial plan, you can use columns B+C and F+G for entering account names and columns D and H for recording the balances. This will leave empty columns to the far left and far right of your page (columns A and I) for visual balance and an empty column down the middle (column E) to separate the two sides of the balance sheet. Let's start with this. You can always add new columns or eliminate extra columns later.

First, enter the basic data. Changes to formats, column widths, and so forth will be done later. Enter the following labels and values:

B7:	**Cash**
B8:	**Accounts receivable**
D7:	**8217.10**
D8:	**94062.28**
F7:	**Accounts payable**
F8:	**Chris McKeon, capital**
H7:	**21665.38**
H8:	**80614.00**

Move to cell D9, click the AutoSum button, and press ENTER. Do the same in cell H9. Your screen should appear as shown in Illustration SP-18.

	A	B	C	D	E	F	G	H
1	Student Name							
2	BAL							
3								
4								
5								
6								
7		Cash		8217.1		Accounts payable		21665.38
8		Accounts receivable		94062.28		Chris McKeon, capital		80614
9				102279.4				102279.4
10								

Illustration SP-18   *Sample Model-Building Worksheet—Stage 1*

In financial statements, dollar signs are usually placed at the top and bottom of columns. For this, the Currency or Accounting number formats are used. If you review Lesson 2 of *Excel Quick* you will be reminded that the Currency format places the dollar sign right next to the number (e.g., $8,217.10) and the Accounting format places the dollar sign to the left side of the cell (e.g., $ 8,217.10). Probably the best format when displaying a column of numbers is Accounting because the dollar signs at the top and bottom will automatically line up.

Move to cell D7, select the Cells command (Format menu), click the Number tab, and pick the Accounting category with two decimals and a dollar sign. Next, move to cell D8 and put it in the Accounting format with two decimals and *no* dollar sign. Finally, move to cell D9 and put it in the Accounting format with two decimals and a dollar sign. You may need to widen column D to view the sum in cell D9.

Repeat these steps applying the Accounting format to the values in column H.

Now use the Borders button to place single underlines in cells D8 and H8, and double underlines in cells D9 and H9. See Illustration SP-19.

	A	B	C	D	E	F	G	H
1	Student Name							
2	BAL							
3								
4								
5								
6								
7		Cash		$ 8,217.10		Accounts payable		$ 21,665.38
8		Accounts receivable		94,062.28		Chris McKeon, capital		80,614.00
9				$ 102,279.38				$ 102,279.38
10								

Illustration SP-19   *Sample Model-Building Worksheet—Stage 2*

It now appears that if you widen columns B and F, you can get rid of columns C and G. It does no harm to leave the extra columns alone, but they are excess baggage. Let's first expand the width of column F. Place the mouse pointer on the line between the column headers F and G at the top of the worksheet. When positioned exactly on the line, the mouse pointer becomes a thick cross with arrowheads at both ends of the horizontal bar. Double-click the mouse button. This action automatically sets column F wide enough to see all the labels in that column. Next, to eliminate column G, click anywhere in column G, select the Delete command (Edit menu) and choose the Entire Column option.

Repeat this process to expand column B and eliminate column C.

Finally, use the mouse (or the Format Column Width command) to narrow the width of column D to about half of its current size. When done, your model should appear as in Illustration SP-20.

	A	B	C	D	E	F
1	Student Name					
2	BAL					
3						
4						
5						
6						
7		Cash	$ 8,217.10		Accounts payable	$ 21,665.38
8		Accounts receivable	94,062.28		Chris McKeon, capital	80,614.00
9			$ 102,279.38			$ 102,279.38
10						

Illustration SP-20   *Sample Model-Building Worksheet—Stage 3*

Looks pretty good! Now for some headings. It does not appear that there are enough empty rows at the top of the statement for these. Let's add three more rows. Select the range A4 to A6 and then choose the Insert Rows command. The first row of the statement is now pushed down to row 10.

The title for the statement will be most visually appealing if it is centered across the columns used in the worksheet. To accomplish this, enter the following labels:

B4:	**Thistle Consulting**
B5:	**Balance Sheet**
B6:	**As of May 31**

Next, select the range B4 to F4 (note: F4 not F6), click the Merge and Center button. This centers "Thistle Consulting" across columns B to F. Repeat this for the range B5 to F5 and then for B6 to F6. This will center each line of the heading above the statement.

Finally, select the range B4 to B6 and click the Bold button. This puts the title in bold print. Move to cell A1 and examine your masterpiece! Your worksheet should appear as shown in Illustration SP-21.

	A	B	C	D	E	F
1	Student Name					
2	BAL					
3						
4			**Thistle Consulting**			
5			**Balance Sheet**			
6			**As of May 31**			
7						
8						
9						
10		Cash	$ 8,217.10		Accounts payable	$ 21,665.38
11		Accounts receivable	94,062.28		Chris McKeon, capital	80,614.00
12			$ 102,279.38			$ 102,279.38
13						

Illustration SP-21   Sample Model-Building Worksheet—Done!

A quick review of the Model-Building Checklist on page 173 will indicate that you have followed most of its suggestions.

The last step is to protect your worksheet. Everything that will remain the same month after month should be protected. Items that will change should be left unprotected. Review the test data provided in the problem statement in Illustration SP-17. From this it is apparent that the account balances will (or could) change each month, as will the date.

To begin the protection process, select cell B6. Then, holding the CTRL key down, also select cells C10, C11, F10, and F11. Next, select the Cells command (Format menu), click the Protection tab, and click the Locked box to deselect it. Click OK. Finally, select the Protection command (Tools menu) and choose the Protect sheet option. Click OK.

Save the file as BAL (File Save As).

Print the file for submission to your instructor (File Print).

TEST DATA SOLUTION

Let's test your model now using the test data from Illustration SP-17. Move to cell B6, press the F2 (EDIT) key, press the BACKSPACE key several times to erase the May date, type **June 30**, and press ENTER. Next, enter all of the June 30 balances in the appropriate cells of the balance sheet. When done, your totals should balance, and they should agree with the check figure for June 30. *The check figure for the June asset total is $96,899.71.*

If you make any corrections to the original file, be sure to save the revised file again as BAL.

When the test data answer agrees with the check figure, the file can be printed again.

ORIGINAL SOLUTION WITH DATA SECTION

Before you leave this lesson, let's discuss what this model might have looked like if a Data Section had been used. Illustration SP-22 presents one possibility. The cells in the range C6 to C9 are unprotected as is cell B16 where the date is entered. Cells C20, C21, F20, and F21 in the Answer Section contain formulas which reference the appropriate cells in the Data Section. The formula in cell C20 is =C6, the formula in cell C21 is =C7, and so forth. This would be a good model design for a bookkeeper who had difficulty keeping assets, liabilities, and equity accounts straight!

	A	B	C	D	E	F
1	Student Name					
2	BAL					
3						
4	Data Section:					
5						
6		Cash	$ 8,217.10			
7		Accounts receivable	94,062.29			
8		Accounts payable	21,665.38			
9		Chris McKeon, capital	80,614.00			
10						
11	Answer Section:					
12						
13						
14			**Thistle Consulting**			
15			**Balance Sheet**			
16			**As of May 31**			
17						
18						
19						
20		Cash	$ 8,217.10		Accounts payable	$ 21,665.38
21		Accounts receivable	94,062.29		Chris McKeon, capital	80,614.00
22			$ 102,279.39			$ 102,279.38
23						

Illustration SP-22   *Sample Model-Building Worksheet with Data Section*

CHART SOLUTION (optional)

Open the file BAL now if it is not already on your screen. The optional chart section (see Illustration SP-17) calls for the creation of a chart based on data found in both months. The easiest way to handle this is to create a Chart Data Table first. The table should not interfere (physically or visually) with the worksheet itself. Let's place it beginning in row 30 using the following steps:

1. Select the Tools Protection command and unprotect the sheet.
2. Use the following table to enter the labels and values in the cells specified (the row and column labels are provided for reference only and should not be keyed). Do not be concerned with the date format Excel uses for your entries on row 31.

	A	B	C
30	**Chart Data**		
31		**May 31**	**June 30**
32	**Cash**	8217.1	31484.2
33	**Accts Rec**	94062.28	65415.51

3. Select the range A31 to C33. Click the Chart Wizard button.
4. Complete the following steps. Step 1—Your first decision is what type of chart you want. Line charts are recommended for showing behaviors over a time period, bar charts are good for comparing different items at the same point in time, and pie charts are used to show the relative proportion of elements that make up a whole. A column chart is what you want in this tickler. Select the column chart and pick the sub-type showing a 3-D Column chart (middle row, left side). Then click Next. Step 2—The current arrangement makes it somewhat difficult to compare May's cash balance with June's and the same for accounts receivable. Try the column orientation. Yes, that's better. Click Next. Step 3—For the Chart title, enter **Asset Balances** in the title box. You could enter a title for the Category (X) axis like "Accounts," but it is already pretty self-evident. Click Next. Step 4—Click Finish.
5. Click the chart once to select it and then double-click the Value (Y) axis. Up pops the Format menu. Click the Number tab and choose the Currency format with no decimal places. Click OK. This places dollar signs on the values on the Y-axis.
6. The dates in row 31 of the Chart Data Table are not really in the format you want. In fact there is no Excel format identical to what you initially entered in those cells. To force Excel to accept your original date entry format, you need to reenter the dates in row 31 placing an *apostrophe* in front of the dates. Do this now.

B31: **'May 31**
C31: **'June 30**

You may recall from Lesson 1 in *Excel Quick* that this is the way to force Excel to accept values and dates as labels. Your completed chart should appear now as shown in Illustration SP-23.

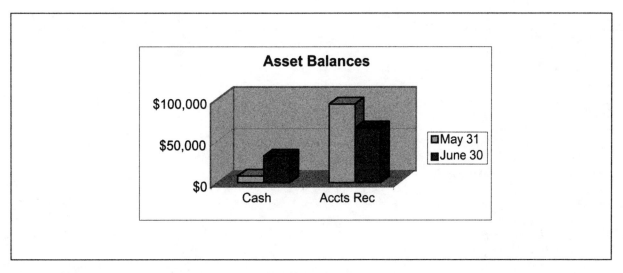

Illustration SP-23   *Sample Model-Building Chart*

7. Reprotect the file using the Tools Protection command.

8. To print a chart, select it (click in an open area on the chart) and choose File Print. Or you can print the worksheet and the chart together by clicking the worksheet and choosing File Print. Do either of these now. Remember, color tends to muddy the printouts on a non-color printer.

9. A chart is saved when the file is saved. Select File Save As now and save the file as BAL, replacing the old version.

After your instructor has reviewed your work, you may erase the file BAL from your Student Disk to make room for future homework files.

P1 ♦ BUSINESS TRANSACTIONS (PTRANS)

LEARNING OBJECTIVES

* Show how financial position is affected by transactions.
* Prepare three basic proprietorship financial statements.
* Back-solve for cash balances.
* Alter the worksheet to accommodate additional transactions.
* Create a chart showing liability and equity categories.

Note: For a problem using the corporate form of business organization, download FTRANS from http://smith.swlearning.com.

PROBLEM DATA

On October 1 of the current year, Justin Clarkson opened Clarkson Talent Agency. The sole proprietorship had the following transactions during October.

a.   Opened a business checking account and made a deposit, $5,000.
b.   Paid rent for October for office space and equipment, $1,000.
c.   Purchased office supplies (stamps, pens, etc.) on account, $680.
d.   Received cash for services rendered, $1,500.
e.   Paid creditor for office supplies purchased on account, $500.
f.   Purchased office supplies for cash, $190.
g.   Billed clients for consultations performed on account, $2,200.
h.   Paid utility bill of $180.
i.   Paid the secretary's salary of $1,200.
j.   Cash was withdrawn for owner's personal use, $500.
k.   Received cash from clients previously billed, $1,500.
l.   Returned $150 of office supplies purchased in transaction f. Received a full refund.

REQUIRED

1.   Review the printout of the worksheet PTRANS. You have been asked to complete the worksheet by recording these transactions.
2.   There are five formulas requested to complete the worksheet. Using the spaces provided below, write the formulas required to complete the worksheet.

FORMULA1_____   FORMULA4_____

FORMULA2_____   FORMULA5_____

FORMULA3_____

3.	Start the spreadsheet program and open the file PTRANS from the Student Disk. Enter the formulas in the appropriate cells on the worksheet. Then enter the increases and decreases resulting from each transaction on the worksheet. For example, the first transaction increases the cash account by $5,000 and also increases the capital account by $5,000. This transaction has already been recorded on the worksheet. The worksheet will automatically total each column as values are entered in that column. When you are finished, check line 26 to make sure that total assets equal total liabilities and equity.

4.	It has been determined that the cost of the supplies used during the month was $300. Record the increase or decrease in the appropriate columns on the worksheet. This is transaction m. Enter your name in cell A1. Save the completed file as PTRANS4. Print the worksheet. Also print your formulas. *Check figure: Ending cash balance (cell B21), $4,580.*

5.	How does transaction m differ from transactions a through l? In other words, why is it treated as a special item?

6. Use the space below to prepare an income statement, a statement of owner's equity, and a balance sheet in good form for Clarkson Talent Agency for the month of October.

WHAT-IF ANALYSIS

7. Justin initially invested $5,000 in the business. Could he have invested less? How little could he have invested initially and never have his cash balance go below zero? To help answer this question, move to column J and analyze the information provided. Then enter different amounts in cell B8 to help determine an answer. When you have determined an answer, use the File Print command to print the range A1 to J21 all on one page. Explain how you derived your answer below.

CHART ANALYSIS

8. Reset cell B8 to $5,000. Click the Chart sheet tab. A pie chart appears on the screen indicating the percentage of each asset in relation to total assets. Justin does not want his cash balance to exceed 60% of his total assets. How much does he have to withdraw at month-end to reduce his cash percentage to 60%? To find out, enter different (negative) values in cell B20 of the worksheet and click the Chart sheet tab after each entry. When you find the withdrawal amount that decreases the cash percentage to 60%, enter that amount in the space provided below.

Withdrawal needed $_____

When the assignment is complete, close the file without saving it again.

TICKLERS (optional)

Worksheet. Two additional transactions occurred in October that need to be recorded on the worksheet.

m. Billed customers for additional services rendered on account, $1,200.
n. Paid creditor for office supplies purchased on account, $120.

Expand the PTRANS4 worksheet to include these transactions. Do not revise column J. Use the Print Preview command (File menu) to make sure that the worksheet will print neatly on one page, then print the worksheet. Save the revised file as PTRANST.

Chart. Using the PTRANS4 file, create a 3-D pie chart that shows the relative balances of the liability and equity accounts. Complete the Chart Tickler Data Table on the Chart worksheet and use it as a basis for preparing the chart. Put your name somewhere on the chart. Save the file again as PTRANS4. Select the chart and then print it out.

	A	B	C	D	E	F	G	H
2				*PTRANS*				
3				*Business Transactions*				
4								
5			Assets		=	Liabilities	+	Equity
6			Accounts	Office		Accounts		Clarkson,
7		Cash	Receivable	Supplies		Payable		Capital
8	a)	$5,000	$0	$0		$0		$5,000
9	b)							
10	c)							
11	d)							
12	e)							
13	f)							
14	g)							
15	h)							
16	i)							
17	j)							
18	k)							
19	l)							
20	m)							
21		*FORMULA1*	*FORMULA2*	*FORMULA3*		*FORMULA4*		*FORMULA5*
22								
23					Balance Verification			
24				Total assets				$0
25				Total liabilities and equity				0
26				Difference				$0
27								

P2 ♦ SERVICE COMPANY WORKSHEET (F1WORK)

LEARNING OBJECTIVES

- Prepare a worksheet for a service firm.
- Prepare financial statements from a worksheet.
- Compare expense levels to national averages.
- Alter the worksheet to include a properly designed income statement.
- Create a chart showing the amount of all expenses.

Note: For a problem using the sole proprietorship form of business organization, download P1WORK from http://smith.swlearning.com.

PROBLEM DATA

The trial balance of Nikki Cleaners at December 31, 2004, the end of the current fiscal year, is below:

Nikki Cleaners
Trial Balance
December 31, 2004

Cash	$ 6,600	
Cleaning Supplies	11,000	
Prepaid Insurance	2,700	
Equipment	103,000	
Accumulated Depreciation		$ 37,050
Accounts Payable		3,720
Common Stock		30,000
Retained Earnings		37,800
Dividends	27,000	
Revenue		77,610
Rent Expense	14,250	
Wages Expense	19,860	
Utilities Expense	1,065	
Miscellaneous Expense	705	
	$186,180	$186,180

Information for the adjusting entries is as follows:

a. Cleaning supplies on hand on December 31, 2004, $9,375.
b. Insurance premiums expired during the year, $900.
c. Depreciation on equipment during the year, $10,800.
d. Wages accrued but not paid at December 31, 2004, $915.

REQUIRED

1. As the accountant for Nikki Cleaners, you have been asked to prepare financial statements for the year. A file called F1WORK has been provided to assist you in this assignment. As you review this file, it should be noted that columns H and I will automatically change when you enter values in columns E or G.

2. There are eight formulas requested to complete the file. Using the spaces provided below, write the formulas required to complete the file.

    FORMULA1_____   FORMULA5_____

    FORMULA2_____   FORMULA6_____

    FORMULA3_____   FORMULA7_____

    FORMULA4_____   FORMULA8_____

3. Start the spreadsheet program and open the file F1WORK from the Student Disk. Enter the formulas in the appropriate cells on the worksheet. Then enter the adjusting amounts in columns E and G. Also, in column D or F, insert the letter corresponding to the adjusting entry (a–d). Column A is "frozen" on the screen to assist you in completing requirement 4.

4. Complete the income statement and balance sheet columns by entering formulas in columns J, K, L, and M that reference the appropriate cells in columns H or I. Net income will be automatically calculated for the income statement and balance sheet. Check to be sure that these numbers are the same. Enter your name in cell A1. Save the completed file as F1WORK4. Print the worksheet. Also print your formulas using landscape orientation and fit-to-1 page scaling. *Check figure: Net income (cell J30), $27,490.*

WHAT-IF ANALYSIS

5. Suppose you discover that an assistant in your department had misunderstood your instructions and had provided you with wrong information on two of the adjusting entries. Cleaning supplies consumed during the year should have been $9,375, and insurance premiums unexpired at year-end were $1,800. Make the corrections on your worksheet and save the corrected file as F1WORK5. Reprint the worksheet.

6. Use the space below to prepare an income statement, a statement of retained earnings, and a balance sheet, using the corrected worksheet (F1WORK5). Assume that no additional owner investments were made during the year.

CHART ANALYSIS

7. With the F1WORK5 file open, click the Chart sheet tab. On the screen, a pie chart shows the percentage composition of the total expenses of Nikki Cleaners. Enter the percentages below. Compare the percentages of Nikki Cleaners with the national statistics provided.

	National Averages	Nikki Cleaners
Rent	12.3%	_____
Utilities	7.7	_____
Wages	33.0	_____
Miscellaneous	1.0	_____
Supplies	17.5	_____
Insurance	4.7	_____
Depreciation	23.8	_____
	100.0%	100.0%

Comment on the differences noted. Why might depreciation, utilities, and rent be so far off from the national percentages? When the assignment is complete, close the file without saving it again.

TICKLERS (optional)

Worksheet. You prepared an income statement in requirement 6. Put a formal income statement somewhere on the F1WORK5 worksheet. Enter formulas in the income statement to reference the appropriate income statement cells in the worksheet. Use proper formats for all value cells. Put your name above the income statement. Print your work (select and print just the income statement cells). Use the Print Preview command (File menu) to make sure that the income statement alone (not the whole worksheet) will print neatly on one page. Save the completed file as F1WORKT.

Chart. Using the F1WORK5 file, create a 3-D column chart showing the dollar total of each of the expenses of Nikki Cleaners. Use the Chart Data Table as a basis for preparing the chart. Use appropriate titles, legends, and formats. Put your name somewhere on the chart. Save the file again as F1WORK5. Select the chart and then print it out.

F1WORK

Service Company Worksheet

Nikki Cleaners
Work Sheet
For Year Ended December 31, 2004

	A	B	C	E F	G	H	I	J	K	L	M
		Trial Balance		Adjustments		Adj. T/Balance		Income Statement		Balance Sheet	
9	Account Title	Dr.	Cr.	Dr.	Cr.	Dr.	Cr.	Dr.	Cr.	Dr.	Cr.
10	Cash	6,600				6,600	0				
11	Cleaning supplies	11,000				11,000	0				
12	Prepaid insurance	2,700				2,700	0				
13	Equipment	103,000				103,000	0				
14	Accumulated depr.		37,050			0	37,050				
15	Accounts payable		3,720			0	3,720				
16	Common stock		30,000			0	30,000				
17	Retained earnings		37,800			0	37,800				
18	Dividends	27,000				27,000	0				
19	Revenue		77,610			0	77,610				
20	Rent expense	14,250				14,250	0				
21	Wages expense	19,860				19,860	0				
22	Utilities expense	1,065				1,065	0				
23	Misc. expense	705				705	0				
24		186,180	186,180								
25	Supplies expense					0	0				
26	Insurance expense					0	0				
27	Depreciation exp.					0	0				
28	Wages payable					0	0				
29				FORM1	FORM2 FORM3 FORM4	FORM5	FORM6	FORM7	FORM8		
30	Net income							0	0	0	0
31								0	0	0	0
32											

41

P3 ◆ MERCHANDISING COMPANY WORKSHEET (P2WORK)

LEARNING OBJECTIVES

- Prepare a worksheet for a merchandising firm.
- Prepare financial statements from a worksheet.
- Compare expense levels to national averages.
- Alter the worksheet to include a properly designed balance sheet.
- Create a chart showing all expenses.

Note: For a problem using the corporate form of business organization, download F2WORK from http://smith.swlearning.com.

PROBLEM DATA

The trial balance of Comtronics at June 30, 2004, the end of the current fiscal year, is as follows:

Comtronics
Trial Balance
June 30, 2004

Cash	$ 6,069	
Accounts Receivable	13,890	
Merchandise Inventory	23,982	
Prepaid Insurance	2,205	
Store Supplies	1,185	
Store Equipment	15,000	
Accumulated Depreciation		$ 1,500
Accounts Payable		6,210
L. Wilson, Capital		41,280
L. Wilson, Drawing	7,200	
Sales		149,700
Purchases	96,450	
Advertising Expense	3,975	
Rent Expense	6,000	
Salaries Expense	19,920	
Utilities Expense	2,814	
	$198,690	$198,690

Adjustment information is as follows:

a. Supplies on hand as of June 30, 2004, $225.
b. Insurance premiums that expired during the year, $1,210.

c. Depreciation on equipment during the year, $750.
d. Salaries accrued but not paid at June 30, 2004, $720.
e. Merchandise inventory on June 30, 2004, $21,932.

REQUIRED

1. As the accountant for Comtronics, you have been asked to prepare adjusting entries, financial statements, and closing entries to complete the accounting cycle for the year. A worksheet called P2WORK has been provided to assist you in this assignment. As you review this worksheet, it should be noted that columns H and I will automatically change when you enter values in columns E and G.

2. There are eight formulas requested to complete the worksheet. Using the spaces provided below, write the formulas required to complete the worksheet.

FORMULA1_____   FORMULA5_____

FORMULA2_____   FORMULA6_____

FORMULA3_____   FORMULA7_____

FORMULA4_____   FORMULA8_____

3. Start the spreadsheet program and open the file P2WORK from the Student Disk. Enter the formulas in the appropriate cells on the worksheet. Then enter the adjusting amounts in columns E and G. Also, in column D or F insert the letter corresponding to the adjusting entry (a—e). (*Note:* Not all textbooks handle the change in inventory as an adjustment. Use the method for handling inventory that is prescribed in your textbook.) Column A is "frozen" on the screen to assist you in completing requirement 4.

4. Complete the income statement and balance sheet by entering formulas in columns J, K, L, and M that reference the appropriate cells in column H or I. Net income will be automatically calculated at the bottom of the income statement and balance sheet columns. Check to be sure that these numbers are the same. Enter your name in cell A1. Save the completed file as P2WORK4. Print the worksheet. Also print your formulas using landscape orientation and fit-to-1 page scaling. *Check figure: Net income (cell J33), $14,851.*

WHAT-IF ANALYSIS

5. You discover that your boss has mistakenly provided you with wrong information on two of the adjusting entries. Expired insurance premiums should have been $1,710, and unpaid salaries should have been $1,220. Make the corrections on your worksheet and save the corrected file as P2WORK5. Reprint the worksheet.

6. In the space provided below and on the following page, prepare an income statement, a capital statement (statement of owner's equity), and a balance sheet. Use the corrected worksheet (P2WORK5) as a basis for your work. Assume no additional owner investments were made during the year.

CHART ANALYSIS

7. Open P2WORK5 and click the Chart sheet tab. On the screen, a pie chart shows the percentage composition of the total expenses of Comtronics. Enter the percentages below.

	National Averages	**Comtronics**
Cost of goods sold	65.0%	_____
Salaries	20.0	_____
Utilities	4.0	_____
Depreciation	4.0	_____
Insurance	3.0	_____
Supplies	2.0	_____
Rent	1.0	_____
Advertising	1.0	_____
	100.0%	100.0%

Compare the percentages of Comtronics with the national statistics provided. Comment on the differences noted. Why might depreciation, utilities, and rent (as a group) be so far off from the national percentages? Any explanation for salaries? COGS? When the assignment is complete, close the file without saving it again.

TICKLERS (optional)

Worksheet. You prepared a balance sheet in requirement 6. Put a formal balance sheet somewhere on the P2WORK5 worksheet. Enter formulas in the income statement to reference the appropriate income statement cells in the worksheet. Use proper formats for all value cells. Put your name above the balance sheet. Print your work (select and print just the balance sheet cells). Use the Print Preview command (File menu) to make sure that the balance sheet alone (not the whole worksheet) will print neatly on one page. Save the completed file as P2WORKT.

Chart. Using the P2WORK5 file, create a column chart showing the dollar total of each of the expenses (except COGS) of Comtronics. Use the Chart Data Table as a basis for preparing the chart. Use appropriate titles, legends, and formats. Put your name somewhere on the chart. Save the file again as P2WORK5. Select the chart and then print it out.

Merchandising Company Worksheet

Comtronics
Work Sheet
For Year Ended June 30, 2004

Account Title	Trial Balance Dr.	Cr.	Adjustments Dr.	Cr.	Adj. T/Balance Dr.	Cr.	Income Statement Dr.	Cr.	Balance Sheet Dr.	Cr.
Cash	6,069				6,069	0				
Accts receivable	13,890				13,890	0				
Merchandise inv.	23,982				23,982	0				
Prepaid insurance	2,205				2,205	0				
Store Supplies	1,185				1,185	0				
Store equipment	15,000				15,000	0				
Accum. deprec.		1,500			0	1,500				
Accounts payable		6,210			0	6,210				
L. Wilson, capital		41,280			0	41,280				
L. Wilson, drawing	7,200				7,200	0				
Sales		149,700			0	149,700				
Purchases	96,450				96,450	0				
Advertising exp.	3,975				3,975	0				
Rent expense	6,000				6,000	0				
Salaries exp.	19,920				19,920	0				
Utilities exp.	2,814				2,814	0				
	198,690	198,690								
Income summary					0	0				
Supplies expense					0	0				
Insurance expense					0	0				
Depreciation exp.					0	0				
Salaries payable					0	0				

FORM1	FORM2	FORM3	FORM4	FORM5	FORM6	FORM7	FORM8

Net income   0   0   0   0
                0   0   0   0

48

P4 ♦ MERCHANDISING COMPANY FINANCIAL STATEMENTS (FMERCH)

LEARNING OBJECTIVES

- Prepare financial statements for a merchandising firm.
- Compare and analyze the change in balances over two months.
- Analyze five-month trends in sales, gross profit, and net income.
- Alter the worksheet by rearranging the order of the Answer Section.
- Create a chart showing the amount of all selling expenses.

Note: For a problem using the sole proprietorship form of business organization, download PMERCH from http://smith.swlearning.com.

PROBLEM DATA

The following information is for Continental Industries for the month ended April 30, 2004:

Accounts Payable	$207,000	Prepaid Insurance	$ 24,000
Accounts Receivable	222,915	Purchases	419,000
Accum. Depreciation—		Purchases Discount	54,325
Store Equipment	304,500	Rent Expense—General	4,500
Advertising Expense	33,000	Rent Expense—Selling	15,000
Cash	53,580	Retained Earnings, beginning	220,000
Common Stock	50,000	Salaries Expense—General	18,000
Depreciation Expense	9,000	Salaries Expense—Selling	96,000
Dividends	144,000	Salaries Payable	12,300
Insurance Expense—General	900	Sales	760,000
Insurance Expense—Selling	8,100	Sales Discount	48,000
Merchandise Inventory, beginning	117,000	Store Equipment	375,000
Merchandise Inventory, ending	155,000	Store Supplies	5,880
		Store Supplies Expense	14,250

REQUIRED

1. Review the worksheet called FMERCH that follows these requirements. You have been asked to prepare Continental's financial statements using this worksheet. Note that the data from the problem have already been entered into the top section of the worksheet. Cells that contain zeros on the worksheet already have formulas entered in them. As you enter formulas onto the worksheet, these zeros will be replaced by values.

2. Using the following spaces provided, write the formulas and titles where requested in the worksheet. FORMULA2 and TITLE A have been written for you as examples.

FORMULA1 _____	FORMULA17 _____
FORMULA2 _____ **=G29** _____	FORMULA18 _____
FORMULA3 _____	FORMULA19 _____
FORMULA4 _____	FORMULA20 _____
FORMULA5 _____	FORMULA21 _____
FORMULA6 _____	FORMULA22 _____
FORMULA7 _____	FORMULA23 _____
FORMULA8 _____	FORMULA24 _____
FORMULA9 _____	FORMULA25 _____
FORMULA10 _____	FORMULA26 _____
FORMULA11 _____	FORMULA27 _____
FORMULA12 _____	FORMULA28_ _____
FORMULA13 _____	FORMULA29 _____
FORMULA14 _____	FORMULA30 _____
FORMULA15 _____	FORMULA31 _____
FORMULA16 _____	FORMULA32 _____
	FORMULA33 _____

TITLE A _____ **Sales Discount** _____	TITLE I _____
TITLE B _____	TITLE J _____
TITLE C _____	TITLE K _____
TITLE D _____	TITLE L _____
TITLE E _____	TITLE M _____
TITLE F _____	TITLE N _____
TITLE G _____	TITLE O _____

TITLE H _____   TITLE P _____

TITLE Q _____   TITLE U _____

TITLE R _____   TITLE V _____

TITLE S _____   TITLE W _____

TITLE T _____   TITLE X _____

                                          TITLE Y _____

3.   Start the spreadsheet program and open the file FMERCH from the Student Disk. Enter all
     formulas and titles where indicated on the worksheet. When you are finished, make sure
     that your balance sheet balances. Enter your name in cell A1. Save your completed file as
     FMERCH3. Print the worksheet. Also print your formulas. *Check figure: Total assets (cell
     G101), $531,875.*

WHAT-IF ANALYSIS

4.   To test your model, enter the following data in the Data Section for the month ended May
     31, 2004.

Accounts Payable	$157,500	Prepaid Insurance	$ 14,175
Accounts Receivable	199,200	Purchases	400,500
Accum. Depreciation—		Purchases Discount	30,000
Store Equipment	316,500	Rent Expense—General	4,500
Advertising Expense	72,000	Rent Expense—Selling	15,000
Cash	37,765	Retained Earnings, beginning	262,575
Common Stock	50,000	Salaries Expense—General	27,000
Depreciation Expense	12,000	Salaries Expense—Selling	120,000
Dividends	127,000	Salaries Payable	6,900
Insurance Expense—General	975	Sales	862,500
Insurance Expense—Selling	8,850	Sales Discount	37,500
Merchandise Inventory, beginning	154,500	Store Equipment	435,000
Merchandise Inventory, ending	93,000	Store Supplies	3,360
		Store Supplies Expense	16,650

     When you are finished, make sure your balance sheet balances. Save your completed file
     as FMERCH4. Reprint the worksheet.

5.   Compare the April and May income statements. Comment on any trends noted.

CHART ANALYSIS

6.   Click the Chart sheet tab on the FMERCH4 file. You will see a chart depicting the five-month trend in sales, gross profit, and net income. What favorable and unfavorable trends do you see in this month-to-month comparison? Comment on any unusual changes.

     When the assignment is complete, close the file without saving it again.

TICKLERS (optional)

Worksheet. Your boss would prefer to have the balance sheet shown before the income statement and the capital statement. Please make this change on the FMERCH4 file. Use the Print Preview command (File menu) to make sure that the worksheet will print neatly on two or three pages, then print the worksheet. Save the completed file as FMERCHT.

Chart. Using the FMERCH4 file, prepare a 3-D pie chart that shows the amount of each of the selling expenses in May. No Chart Data Table is needed. Select A56 to A61 as one range on the worksheet to be charted and then hold down the CTRL key and select E56 to E61 as the second range. Put your name somewhere on the chart. Save the file again as FMERCH4. Select the chart and then print it out.

	A	B	C	D	E	F	G
2				**FMERCH**			
3			*Merchandising Company Financial Statements*				
4							
5	Data Section					Month:	April 30, 2004
6							
7	Accounts Payable						$207,000
8	Accounts Receivable						222,915
9	Accumulated Depreciation-Store Equipment						304,500
10	Advertising Expense						33,000
11	Cash						53,580
12	Common Stock						50,000
13	Depreciation Expense-Store Equipment						9,000
14	Dividends						144,000
15	Insurance Expense-General						900
16	Insurance Expense-Selling						8,100
17	Merchandise Inventory, beginning						117,000
18	Merchandise Inventory, ending						155,000
19	Prepaid Insurance						24,000
20	Purchases						419,000
21	Purchases Discount						54,325
22	Rent Expense-General						4,500
23	Rent Expense-Selling						15,000
24	Retained Earnings, beginning						220,000
25	Salaries Expense-General						18,000
26	Salaries Expense-Selling						96,000
27	Salaries Payable						12,300
28	Sales						760,000
29	Sales Discount						48,000
30	Store Equipment						375,000
31	Store Supplies						5,880
32	Store Supplies Expense						14,250
33							

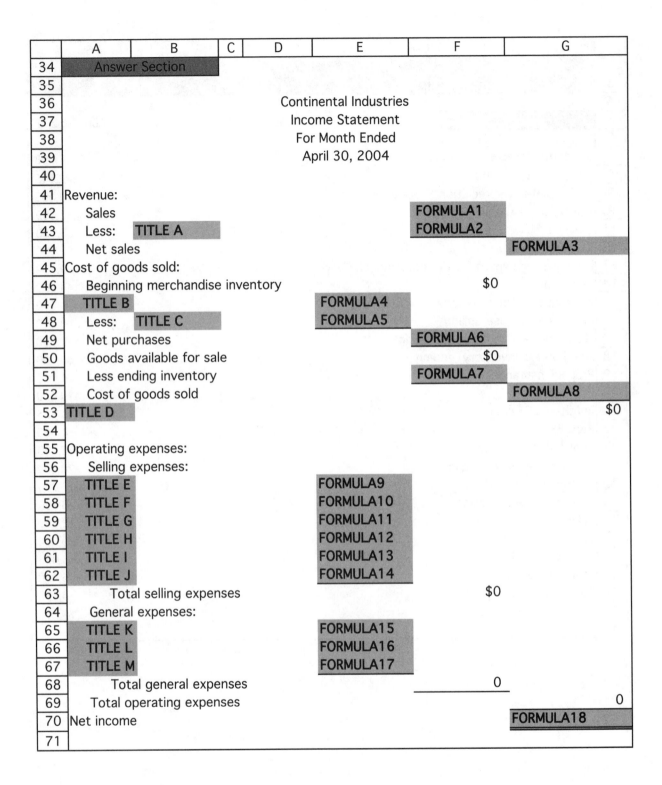

	A	B	C	D	E	F	G
34	Answer Section						
35							
36					Continental Industries		
37					Income Statement		
38					For Month Ended		
39					April 30, 2004		
40							
41	Revenue:						
42	Sales					FORMULA1	
43	Less:	TITLE A				FORMULA2	
44	Net sales						FORMULA3
45	Cost of goods sold:						
46	Beginning merchandise inventory					$0	
47	TITLE B				FORMULA4		
48	Less:	TITLE C			FORMULA5		
49	Net purchases					FORMULA6	
50	Goods available for sale					$0	
51	Less ending inventory					FORMULA7	
52	Cost of goods sold						FORMULA8
53	TITLE D						$0
54							
55	Operating expenses:						
56	Selling expenses:						
57	TITLE E				FORMULA9		
58	TITLE F				FORMULA10		
59	TITLE G				FORMULA11		
60	TITLE H				FORMULA12		
61	TITLE I				FORMULA13		
62	TITLE J				FORMULA14		
63	Total selling expenses					$0	
64	General expenses:						
65	TITLE K				FORMULA15		
66	TITLE L				FORMULA16		
67	TITLE M				FORMULA17		
68	Total general expenses					0	
69	Total operating expenses						0
70	Net income						FORMULA18
71							

	A	B	C	D	E	F	G
72							
73				Continental Industries			
74				Statement of Retained earnings			
75				For Month Ended			
76				April 30, 2004			
77							
78	Beginning balance						FORMULA19
79	Net income					FORMULA20	
80	TITLE N					FORMULA21	
81	Change in equity					FORMULA22	
82	Ending balance						$0
83							
84							
85				Continental Industries			
86				Balance Sheet			
87				April 30, 2004			
88							
89				Assets			
90	Current assets:						
91	TITLE O					FORMULA23	
92	TITLE P					FORMULA24	
93	TITLE Q					FORMULA25	
94	TITLE R					FORMULA26	
95	TITLE S					FORMULA27	
96	Total current assets						$0
97	Fixed assets:						
98	TITLE T					FORMULA28	
99	TITLE U					FORMULA29	
100	Total fixed assets						0
101	Total assets						$0
102							
103				Liabilities & Stockholders' Equity			
104	Liabilities:						
105	TITLE V					FORMULA30	
106	TITLE W					FORMULA31	
107	Total liabilities						$0
108	Stockholders' Equity:						
109	TITLE X					FORMULA32	
110	TITLE Y					FORMULA33	0
111	Total liabilities & stockholders' equity						$0
112							

P5 ◆ BANK RECONCILIATION (BANKREC)

LEARNING OBJECTIVES

- Prepare a bank reconciliation and the necessary adjusting journal entries.
- Prepare a bank reconciliation with incomplete data.
- Interpret differences between book and bank balances.
- Alter the file to accept additional outstanding checks.
- Create a chart plotting book and bank balances.

PROBLEM DATA

Altech Industries deposits all receipts in a night depository after banking hours. The data needed to reconcile the bank statement as of October 31, 2004, have been extracted from records and are as follows:

From Altech's records:

Checking account balance as of September 30	$8,720.23
Cash received and deposited in October (detail below*)	4,735.45
Checks written during October (detail below**)	–4,828.88
Checkbook balance as of October 31	$8,626.80

*Date and amount of each deposit in October: Oct. 3, $545.25; Oct. 8, $842.00; Oct. 11, $978.35; Oct. 16, $658.05; Oct. 19, $643.90; Oct. 24, $352.62; Oct. 28, $715.28.

**Number and amount of each check issued in October:

No.	Amount	No.	Amount	No.	Amount	No.	Amount
750	$361.90	754	$869.52	758	$246.60	762	$236.74
751	64.71	755	471.86	759	Void	763	Void
752	462.18	756	156.20	760	87.95	764	210.00
753	51.90	757	274.35	761	719.27	765	615.70

From October's bank statement:

Balance as of September 30	$ 9,568.63
Deposits recorded in October (detail below*)	4,382.07
Checks charged to account in October (detail below**)	– 4,180.93
Other adjustments (detail below***)	1,387.80
Balance as of October 31	$11,157.57

*Date and amount of each deposit in October: Oct. 1, $361.90; Oct. 4, $545.25; Oct. 9, $842.00; Oct. 12, $978.35; Oct. 17, $658.05; Oct. 20, $643.90; Oct. 25, $352.62.

**Number and amount of each check in October:

No.	Amount	No.	Amount	No.	Amount	No.	Amount
740	$ 90.60	751	$ 64.71	755	$471.86	758	$264.60
747	217.45	752	462.18	756	156.20	760	87.95
748	570.97	753	51.90	757	274.35	762	236.74
750	361.90	754	869.52				

***Description of each memo accompanying October's bank statement:

Date	Description	Amount
Oct. 4	Bank debit memo for check returned because of insufficient funds	$ 64.20
Oct. 12	Bank credit memo for note collected:	
	Principal	1,400.00
	Interest	60.00
Oct. 30	Bank debit memo for service charges	8.00

REQUIRED

1. As treasurer, you have been asked to prepare a bank reconciliation as of October 31. Review the file called BANKREC that follows these requirements. The bank reconciliation as of September 30 is provided for you as a sample completed worksheet. You may need to refer to the September 30 bank reconciliation for information on outstanding checks.

2. Using the spaces provided below, write the formulas where requested in the file. Carefully review the September 30 printout and note that subtractions are entered as negative numbers.

   FORMULA1_____   FORMULA3_____

   FORMULA2_____

3. Start the spreadsheet program and open the file BANKREC from the Student Disk. Enter the formulas where indicated on the worksheet. Prepare a bank reconciliation as of October 31. Assume that all errors are the depositor's fault. Checks 754–757 were for salaries; all other checks were payments to suppliers on account. The reconciliation is not complete until the difference between the adjusted balances (cell C45) is zero. Enter your name in cell A1. Save your completed file as OCT31. Print the worksheet. Also print your formulas. *Check figure: Adjusted balance (cell E25), $9,996.60.*

4. In the space provided below, prepare the necessary adjusting journal entries.

58

WHAT-IF ANALYSIS

5. Erase all October data and use the worksheet to complete the following bank reconciliation at November 30, 2004:

Adjusted balance	$7,608
Balance per bank	7,950
Balance per books	?
Checks outstanding	547
Deposits in transit	?
Service charges	16

Save your completed file as NOV30. Print the worksheet.

CHART ANALYSIS

6. Open the OCT31 file. Click the Chart sheet tab. On the screen, a column chart appears illustrating relative book and bank balances at July 31 and August 31. In the space provided below, list at least two reasons why the discrepancy between book and bank balances may have existed at July 31.

a.

b.

Why may it have existed at August 31?

a.

b.

When the assignment is complete, close the file without saving it again.

TICKLERS (optional)

Worksheet. Suppose that there are ten checks outstanding at the end of December 2004. Modify the BANKREC worksheet to accept additional outstanding checks. Put your name in cell A1. Use the Print Preview command (File menu) to make sure that the worksheet will print neatly on one page, then print the worksheet. Save the completed file as BANKRECT.

Chart. Using the OCT31 file, prepare a line chart to show both the monthly ending bank balance and the adjusted book balance from July 31 through November 30. Use the Chart Data Table as a basis for preparing the chart. Expand the table to include data for September, October, and November based on the information provided in the problem. Put your name somewhere on the chart. Save the file again as OCT31. Select the chart and then print it out.

	A	B	C
2		*BANKREC*	
3		*Bank Reconciliation*	
4			
5		Altech Industries	
6		Bank Reconciliation	
7		October 31, 2004	
8			
9			
10	Balance per bank statement		$0.00
11			
12	Additions by depositor not on bank statement:		
13			
14			
15			
16	Deductions by depositor not on bank statement:		
17			
18			
19			
20			
21			
22			
23	Bank errors:		
24			
25	Adjusted balance		FORMULA1
26			
27			
28	Balance per books		$0.00
29			
30	Additions by bank not recorded by depositor:		
31			
32			
33			
34	Deductions by bank not recorded by depositor:		
35			
36			
37			
38			
39			
40	Depositor's errors:		
41			
42	Adjusted balance		FORMULA2
43			
44			
45	Difference between adjusted balances		FORMULA3
46			

	A	B	C
2		*BANKREC*	
3		*Bank Reconciliation*	
4			
5		Altech Industries	
6		Bank Reconciliation	
7		September 30, 2004	
8			
9			
10	Balance per bank statement		$9,568.63
11			
12	Additions by depositor not on bank statement:		
13		Deposit in transit 9/30	361.90
14			
15			
16	Deductions by depositor not on bank statement:		
17		Checks outstanding	
18		740	(90.60)
19		747	(217.45)
20		748	(570.97)
21		749	(331.28)
22			
23	Bank errors:		
24			
25	Adjusted balance		*$8,720.23*
26			
27			
28	Balance per books		$8,728.23
29			
30	Additions by bank not recorded by depositor:		
31			
32			
33			
34	Deductions by bank not recorded by depositor:		
35		Service charge	(8.00)
36			
37			
38			
39			
40	Depositor's errors:		
41			
42	Adjusted balance		*$8,720.23*
43			
44			
45	Difference between adjusted balances		*$0.00*
46			

P6 ♦ AGING ACCOUNTS RECEIVABLE (AGING)

LEARNING OBJECTIVES

* Prepare an accounts receivable aging schedule.
* Apply the allowance method of accounting for uncollectible accounts.
* Interpret changes in collection patterns.
* Alter the file to include one additional customer.
* Create a chart showing estimated uncollectible balances by age category.

PROBLEM DATA

On October 31, 2004, Allure Beauty Supplies had the following amounts due from its customers:

Customer	Total	Not Yet Due	1–30 Days Past Due	31–60 Days Past Due	61–90 Days Past Due	Over 90 Days Past Due
A Cut Above	$ 1,800	$1,300	$ 350			$150
Beauty Box	3,750	2,800	950			
Bush Whackers	5,000	1,500	1,500	$1,000	$1,000	
Curl & Swirl	1,900	1,900				
Cut Loose	400					400
Hair Affair	1,750		500	320	700	230
Totals	$14,600	$7,500	$3,300	$1,320	$1,700	$780

Based on the company's past experience, it has established the following percentages for estimating uncollectible accounts:

Age Interval	Percent Uncollectible
Not yet due	1%
1–30 days past due	3
31–60 days past due	5
61–90 days past due	10
Over 90 days past due	25

REQUIRED

1. You have been asked to estimate the total amount of uncollectible accounts expense as of October 31 by completing the file called AGING.

2. Using the spaces provided below, write the formulas where requested in the file. FORMULA1 has been done for you as an example.

    FORMULA1 _____ **=D21** _____   FORMULA7 _____

    FORMULA2 _____   FORMULA8 _____

    FORMULA3 _____   FORMULA9 _____

    FORMULA4 _____   FORMULA10 _____

    FORMULA5 _____   FORMULA11 _____

    FORMULA6 _____   FORMULA12 _____

3. Start the spreadsheet program and open the file AGING from the file disk. Enter all formulas where indicated on the worksheet. Enter your name in cell A1. Save your completed file as AGING3. Print the worksheet. Also print your formulas. *Check figure: Total uncollectible (cell F28), $605*

4. Assume that October's credit sales were $35,000. In the spaces provided below, record the journal entry for the provision for uncollectible accounts under each of the following independent assumptions:

    a. The Allowance for Doubtful Accounts before adjustment has a credit balance of $500.

    b. The Allowance for Doubtful Accounts before adjustment has a debit balance of $250.

    c. Uncollectible accounts expense is estimated at 2% of sales.

WHAT-IF ANALYSIS

5. Erase the aging information for October and enter the following information for November 30, 2004:

Customer	Total	Not Yet Due	1–30 Days Past Due	31–60 Days Past Due	61–90 Days Past Due	Over 90 Days Past Due
A Cut Above	$ 2,850	$ 1,700	$ 800	$ 350		
Alley Cuts	2,500	2,500				
Bush Whackers	6,500	1,500	1,500	1,500	$1,000	$1,000
Cut Loose	400					400
Hair Affair	3,020	1,500		500	320	700
Shear Heaven	8,900	8,900				
Totals	$24,170	$16,100	$2,300	$2,350	$1,320	$2,100

Save the results as AGING5. Print the worksheet. Has the estimated total uncollectible accounts increased or decreased in November? Explain.

CHART ANALYSIS

6. a. With AGING5 still on the screen, click the Chart sheet tab. Describe what is being plotted out on this chart.

   b. Open the AGING3 file and click the Chart sheet tab. Compare the pattern of this chart to the one for AGING5. Note any trends below.

   When the assignment is complete, close the files without saving them again.

TICKLERS (optional)

Worksheet. Suppose that there had been one additional customer with a balance due at November 30. This customer was Totally Clips, and it owed $1,300 which was not yet due. Alter the AGING5 worksheet to allow entry of this information and modify any affected formulas. Use the Print Preview command (File menu) to make sure that the worksheet will print neatly on one page, then print the worksheet. Save the completed file as AGINGT.

Chart. Using the AGING3 file, develop a 3D column chart to show the total estimated uncollectible amounts (in dollars) for each age category. No chart data table is needed; use B23 to B27 as the X-Axis (or make up your own labels) and then holding down the CTRL key select F23 to F27 as the range of values to be plotted. Put your name somewhere on the chart. Save the file again as AGING3. Print the chart.

	A	B	C	D	E	F	G
2				*AGING*			
3				*Aging Accounts Receivable*			
4							
5					Date:	October 31, 2004	
6							
7				Analysis of Accounts Receivable by Age			
8			Not	1-30	31-60	61-90	Over 90
9			Yet	Days	Days	Days	Days
10	Customer	Total	Due	Past Due	Past Due	Past Due	Past Due
11	A Cut Above	$1,800	$1,300	$350			$150
12	Beauty Box	3,750	2,800	950			
13	Bush Whackers	5,000	1,500	1,500	1,000	1,000	
14	Curl & Swirl	1,900	1,900				
15	Cut Loose	400					400
16	Hair Affair	1,750		500	320	700	230
17	Totals	$14,600	$7,500	$3,300	$1,320	$1,700	$780
18							
19				Estimate of Probable			
20				Uncollectible Accounts Expense			
21				Total	Percent	Total	
22				Amount	Uncoll.	Uncoll.	
23		Not yet due		FORMULA1	1%	FORMULA7	
24		1-30 days past due		FORMULA2	3%	FORMULA8	
25		31-60 days past due		FORMULA3	5%	FORMULA9	
26		61-90 days past due		FORMULA4	10%	FORMULA10	
27		Over 90 days past due		FORMULA5	25%	FORMULA11	
28		Totals		FORMULA6		FORMULA12	
29							

66

P7 ◆ INVENTORY COST FLOW ASSUMPTIONS (FIFOLIFO)

LEARNING OBJECTIVES

- Calculate the cost of goods sold and ending inventory using the specific identification, FIFO, LIFO, and weighted average methods.
- Contrast the effect of each on income determination, taxes, and cash flow during periods of inflation, deflation, and stable prices.
- Identify the source and effect of inventory ("fictitious") profits.
- Identify the effect of last minute purchases on income determination.

PROBLEM DATA

Del Rio began Rio Enterprises on January 1 with 200 units of inventory. During the year 500 additional units were purchased, 500 units were sold, and Del ended the year with 200 units. Del is very satisfied with his first year of business although the cost of replacing his inventory rose continually throughout the year. The 500 units sold for a total of $320,000 and the 500 units purchased to replace them cost $256,000, so his cash account has increased by $64,000. Del is concerned however because he has three obligations yet to meet: taxes, dividends, and his wife. Federal and state income taxes will take 40% of his income. His investors are to receive dividends equal to half of any income after taxes are paid. And finally, Del promised his wife a big trip to Hawaii if she let him quit his job as a professor and start his own business. He promised her he'd "make at least $50,000 after taxes. That will give us $25,000 after paying off the investors."

Del kept fairly good records during the year and knows the specific cost of each inventory unit sold. He has prepared the following table to summarize his purchases and sales.

Purchase Date	Unit Quantity	Unit Cost	Total Cost	Specific Units Sold	Cost of Units Sold
Beginning	200	$400	$ 80,000	200	$ 80,000
Mar. 7	100	$440	$ 44,000	50	22,000
May 13	50	480	24,000		
Aug. 28	200	520	104,000	200	104,000
Nov. 20	150	560	84,000	50	28,000
Total purchased	500		256,000		
Total available	700		$336,000		
Sales	500			500	$234,000
Ending balance	200				

A quick calculation shows that Rio's net income will be $51,600 using specific costs for the inventory sold. Sales minus cost of goods sold equals gross profit ($320,000 − $234,000 = $86,000). Taxes to be paid are 40% ($86,000 × .4 = $34,400). Subtract taxes from gross profit to get net income ($86,000 − $34,400 = $51,600).

Next, Del calculates his ending cash balance. He currently has $64,000 from his sales less his inventory replacement purchases ($320,000 − $256,000 = $64,000). He needs to pay taxes ($34,400) and dividends to his investors ($51,600 × .5 = $25,800). Subtracting $34,400 and $25,800 from $64,000 leaves him with only $3,800. Yikes!

Del is shocked by the computations. He cannot figure out how he will ever explain to his wife that he has net income in excess of $50,000 and yet after paying off the investors he will have only $3,800 to show for it! Del knows you are taking an accounting class and comes to you for help.

REQUIRED

1. Del has heard that the choice of an inventory cost flow assumption can have a significant effect on net income and taxes. He asks you to show him the differences between the specific identification method and the cost flow assumptions of FIFO, LIFO, and weighted average. Review the worksheet FIFOLIFO that follows these requirements. Note that all of the problem data have been entered in the Data Section of the worksheet.

2. Using a pencil, fill in columns F and G in the Data Section of the worksheet printout at the end of this problem.

3. Use the spaces provided below to write the formulas for each of the cells requested in the worksheet. Be careful to write FORMULAs 1 through 8 broadly enough to include different sales quantities (i.e., suppose all inventory was sold, or no inventory was sold).

FORMULA1_____   FORMULA8_____

FORMULA2_____   FORMULA9_____

FORMULA3_____   FORMULA10_____

FORMULA4_____   FORMULA11_____

FORMULA5_____   FORMULA12_____

FORMULA6_____   FORMULA13_____

FORMULA7_____   FORMULA14_____

4. Start the spreadsheet program and open the file FIFOLIFO from the Student Disk. Fill in columns F and G in the Data Section. Then enter all 14 formulas where indicated on the worksheet. Enter your name in cell A1. Save the results as FIFOLIF4. Print the worksheet when done. Also print your formulas. *Check figure: FIFO net income (cell E36), $56,400.*

5. Examine your completed worksheet and answer the following questions:

   a. Which inventory cost flow assumption produces the most net income?

   b. Which inventory cost flow assumption produces the least net income?

   c. What caused the difference between your answers to a and b?

   d. Which inventory cost flow assumption produces the highest ending cash balance?

   e. Which inventory cost flow assumption produces the lowest ending cash balance?

   f. Does the assumption that produces the highest net income also produce the highest cash balance? Explain.

   g. As you recall, Del originally used the specific identification method in his initial calculations when he projected $51,600 net income. According to Del's reckoning that should have left him cash of $25,800 (50% of $51,600) after paying his investors. Why would he only have $3,800 left? Explain.

   h. Which inventory cost flow assumption would you suggest Del use? Explain.

WHAT-IF ANALYSIS

6. What changes would have taken place if Del's purchase prices had fallen rather than risen? To find out, enter the following values in cells C11 through C14, respectively: $390, 380, 370, and 360. Print the results. Explain what the changes are and why they have taken place.

7. Suppose Del's purchase prices had remained constant. Enter $400 in cells C11 through C14. Explain what changes take place and why.

8. Reset the purchase prices to their original values (cells C11 through C14). Suppose Del had purchased 250 units on November 20 rather than 150. Enter 250 in cell C14 and alter column G in the Data Section. Explain what happens to net income under each inventory cost flow assumption and why. Also, what "management" implications might this have for Del?

9. Reset the November 20 purchase to 150 units including column G. To test your formulas, suppose that Del had sold 600 units rather than 500. Sales now total $384,000. The extra units sold come from the May 13 purchase (25 units) and the November 20 purchase (75 units). Change cell B17 to 600 and cells D32 through G32 to $384,000. Alter columns E, F, and G in the Data Section to reflect the change. Your formulas should automatically redo the Calculations and Answer Sections. Print the results again.

CHART ANALYSIS

10. Close the file without saving and open it again (FIFOLIF4). Click the Chart sheet tab. On the screen is a column chart showing ending inventory costs. During a deflationary period, which bar (A, B, or C) represents FIFO costing, which represents LIFO costing, and which represents weighted average? Explain your reasoning.

When the assignment is complete, close the file without saving it again.

TICKLERS (optional)

Worksheet. On January 4 following year-end, Rio Enterprises received a shipment of 60 units of product costing $580 each. These units had been ordered by Del in December and had been shipped to him on December 27. They were shipped F.O.B. shipping point. Revise the FIFOLIF4 worksheet to include this shipment. Use the Print Preview command (File menu) to make sure that the worksheet will print neatly on one page, then print the worksheet. Save the completed file as FIFOLIFT.

Chart. Using the FIFOLIF4 file, prepare a 3D bar (stacked) chart showing the cost of goods sold and ending inventory under each of the four inventory cost flow assumptions. No Chart Data Table is needed. Use the values in the Calculations Section of the worksheet for your chart. Put your name somewhere on the chart. Save the file again as FIFOLIF4. Print the chart.

	A	B	C	D	E	F	G
2				FIFOLIFO			
3				Inventory Cost Flow Assumptions			
4							
5	Data Section						
6							
7					Specific	FIFO	LIFO
8	Purchase	Unit	Unit	Total	Units	Units	Units
9	Date	Quantity	Cost	Cost	Sold	Sold	Sold
10	Beginning Balance	200	$400	$80,000	200		
11	Mar 7	100	$440	$44,000	50		
12	May 13	50	480	24,000			
13	Aug 28	200	520	104,000	200		
14	Nov 20	150	560	84,000	50		
15	Total purchased	500		256,000			
16	Total available	700		$336,000			
17	Sales	500			500	0	0
18	Ending balance	200			these totals must agree		
19					with cell B17		
20							
21	Calculations						
22							
23				Specific	FIFO	LIFO	Average
24	Cost of goods sold			FORM1	FORM2	FORM3	FORM4
25	Ending inventory cost			FORM5	FORM6	FORM7	FORM8
26	Total goods available			$0	$0	$0	$0
27				these totals must agree with cell D16			
28	Answer Section						
29							
30					Income Statement		
31				Specific	FIFO	LIFO	Average
32	Sales			$320,000	$320,000	$320,000	$320,000
33	Cost of goods sold			FORM9	FORM10	0	0
34	Gross profit			FORM11	FORM12	$0	$0
35	Taxes (40%)			FORM13	FORM14	0	0
36	Net income			$0	$0	$0	$0
37							
38							
39					Cash Flow Analysis		
40				Specific	FIFO	LIFO	Average
41	Sales			$320,000	$320,000	$320,000	$320,000
42	Less inventory replacement			(256,000)	(256,000)	(256,000)	(256,000)
43				$64,000	$64,000	$64,000	$64,000
44	Less taxes			0	0	0	0
45	Less dividends			0	0	0	0
46	Change in cash account			$0	$0	$0	$0
47							

P8 ◆ GROSS PROFIT METHOD (GP)

LEARNING OBJECTIVES

- Use the gross profit method to estimate ending inventory.
- Identify reasons for differences between book and physical inventories.
- Interpret trends in the gross profit ratio.
- Alter the worksheet to include a new input category.
- Create a chart demonstrating the relationship between gross profit percentage and estimated ending inventory.

PROBLEM DATA

On September 30, 2004, the general ledger of O'Connor's Sunrise Shop, which uses the calendar year as its accounting period, showed the following year-to-date account balances:

Sales	$325,000
Sales returns and allowances	8,500
Purchases	300,000
Purchases returns and allowances	11,000

The merchandise inventory account had a $47,525 balance on January 1, 2004. The historical gross profit percentage is 40%.

REQUIRED

1. O'Connor's prepares quarterly financial statements and takes physical inventory once a year—at the end of the accounting period. In order to prepare the financial statements for the third quarter, the store needs to have an estimate of ending inventory. You have been asked to use the gross profit method to estimate the ending inventory. Review the worksheet called GP. Study it carefully because it may have a solution format somewhat different from the one shown in your textbook.

2. Using the spaces provided below, write the formulas where requested in the worksheet.

FORMULA1_____   FORMULA5_____

FORMULA2_____   FORMULA6_____

FORMULA3_____   FORMULA7_____

FORMULA4_____

3. Start the spreadsheet program and open the file GP from the Student Disk. Enter all the formulas where indicated on the worksheet. Enter your name in cell A1. Save your completed worksheet as GP3. Print the worksheet. Also print your formulas. *Check figure: Estimated ending inventory (cell D22), $146,625.*

WHAT-IF ANALYSIS

4. On December 31, 2004, the year-to-date account balances of selected accounts were as follows:

Sales	$495,000
Sales returns and allowances	13,000
Purchases	330,000
Purchases returns and allowances	15,000

Estimated ending merchandise inventory at December 31, 2004 is $_____.

5. A physical count of merchandise inventory on December 31, 2004 revealed inventory costing $68,500. In the space below, list at least two possible reasons for this balance to be different from the estimate in Requirement 4.

CHART ANALYSIS

6. Click the Chart sheet tab. The line chart that appears plots quarterly sales and gross profit for all four quarters. Examine the pattern of behavior for these two items and comment on any favorable or unfavorable trends noted. What is happening to the gross profit ratio?

When the assignment is complete, close the file without saving it again.

TICKLERS (optional)

Worksheet. At the present time, O'Connor's Sunrise Shop includes payments for freight costs in the purchases account. On the advice of an accountant, O'Connor's Sunrise Shop will establish a separate account for freight-in charges (also called transportation-in) in 2005. Modify the GP3 worksheet to accept this additional item of input. Then estimate ending merchandise inventory at March 31, 2005 using the following data:

Sales	$150,000
Sales returns and allowances	3,750
Purchases	112,500
Purchases returns and allowances	4,800
Freight-in	1,100
Beginning inventory (12/31/04)	68,500
Gross profit percent (historical)	39%

Use the Print Preview command (File menu) to make sure that the worksheet will print neatly on one page, then print the worksheet. Save the completed file as GPT.

Chart. Using the GP3 file, create an XY chart for the GP3 worksheet that demonstrates the relationship between gross profit percentage (X-axis) and estimated ending inventory (Y-axis). Complete the Chart Tickler Data Table and use it as a basis for preparing the chart. Put your name somewhere on the chart. Save the file again as GP3. Print the chart.

	A	B	C	D
2	*GP*			
3	*Gross Profit*			
4				
5	Data Section			
6				
7	Sales		$325,000	
8	Sales returns and allowances		8,500	
9	Purchases		300,000	
10	Purchases returns and allowances		11,000	
11	Beginning inventory		47,525	
12	Gross profit percent (historical)		40%	
13				
14	Answer Section			
15				
16	Beginning inventory			FORMULA1
17	Net purchases			FORMULA2
18	Cost of goods available for sale			FORMULA3
19	Net sales		FORMULA4	
20	Estimated gross profit (in dollars)		FORMULA5	
21	Estimated cost of goods sold			FORMULA6
22	Estimated ending inventory			FORMULA7
23				

P9 ◆ DEPRECIATION (DEPREC)

LEARNING OBJECTIVES

- Compute depreciation using the straight-line, units of production, and double-declining balance methods.
- Identify patterns of depreciation over an asset's life.
- Interpret patterns of accumulated depreciation over an asset's life.
- Alter the worksheet to allow for the computation of partial year depreciation.
- Create a chart plotting annual depreciation under all three depreciation methods.

PROBLEM DATA

Picqua Production Company recently acquired a new machine at a cost of $266,000. The machine has an estimated useful life of four years or 100,000 hours, and a salvage value of $26,000. This machine will be used 20,000 hours during Year 1, 30,000 hours in Year 2, 40,000 hours in Year 3, and 10,000 hours in Year 4.

REQUIRED

1. Picqua buys equipment frequently and wants to print a depreciation schedule for each asset's life. Review the worksheet called DEPREC that follows these requirements. Since some assets acquired are depreciated by straight-line, others by units of production, and others by double-declining-balance, DEPREC shows all three methods. You are to use this worksheet to prepare depreciation schedules for the new machine.

2. Using the spaces provided below, write the formulas requested. Be sure to use cell references wherever possible in your formulas instead of numbers. You should find the year numbers in column B helpful for some formulas. Your instructor will tell you whether you are to (1) construct your own formulas or (2) use =SLN and =DDB. FORMULA1 has been written both ways for you as an example. Assume that all assets acquired will have at least a three-year life. Note that all cells on the worksheet containing zeros have been preprogrammed to perform depreciation calculations.

FORMULA1 __=(D7-D8)/D9 or =SLN(D7,D8,D9)__   FORMULA5_____

FORMULA2_____   FORMULA6_____

FORMULA3_____   FORMULA7_____

FORMULA4_____   FORMULA8_____

FORMULA9_____   FORMULA11_____

FORMULA10_____   FORMULA12_____

3.   Start the spreadsheet program and open the file DEPREC from the file disk. Enter the formulas in the appropriate cells. Does your depreciation total $240,000 under all three methods? If not, correct your error. *Hint:* If your double-declining-balance method is off, check cell E32 where FORMULA12 is located. It should include an =IF statement that will enter a modified calculation of depreciation if Year 4 is the last year of the asset's expected life. Enter your name in cell A1. Save the completed file as DEPREC3. Print the worksheet. Also print your formulas using landscape orientation and fit-to-1 page scaling. *Check figure: DDB depreciation for Year 3 (cell E31), $33,250.*

4.   In the space below, prepare the journal entry to record the depreciation taken in Year 3 under the units of production method.

WHAT-IF ANALYSIS

5.   To test your formulas, assume the machine purchased had an estimated useful life of three years (20,000, 30,000, and 50,000 hours, respectively). Enter the new information in the Data Section of the worksheet. Does your depreciation total $240,000 under all three methods?

There are three common errors made by students completing this worksheet. Let's clear up two of them. One, an asset that has a three-year life should have no depreciation claimed in Year 4. This can be corrected using an =IF statement in Year 4. See Appendix A of *Excel Quick* for a discussion of this =function. For example, the correct formula in cell C32 is IF(B32>D9,0,(D7-D8)/D9) or IF(B32>D9,0,SLN(D7,D8,D9)). You may wish to edit what you have already entered rather than retype it.

Two, as mentioned in Requirement 3, the double-declining-balance calculation needs to be modified in the last year of the asset's life. Assuming you have already modified the formula for Year 4 (per instructions in Step 3), alter the formula for Year 3 also.

If you corrected any formulas, test their correctness by trying different estimated useful lives (between 3 and 8) in cell E9. Then reset the Data Section to the original values, save the revised file as DEPREC3, and reprint the worksheet to show the correct formulas.

The third common error doesn't need to be corrected in this problem. The general form of the double-declining-balance formula needs to be modified to check the net book value of the asset each year to make sure it does not go below salvage value. =DDB does this automatically, but if you are writing your own formulas this gets very complicated and is beyond the scope of the problem.

6. A truck was recently purchased for $33,000 with a salvage value of $5,000 and an estimated useful life of eight years or 150,000 miles (24,000 miles per year for the first five years and 10,000 miles per year after that). Enter the new information in the Data Section of the worksheet. Again make sure the totals for all three methods are in agreement. Print the worksheet. Save this new data as DEPREC6.

CHART ANALYSIS

7. Open the DEPREC6 file. Click the Chart sheet tab. This chart shows the accumulated depreciation under all three depreciation methods. Identify below the depreciation method that each represents.

Series 1 _____

Series 2 _____

Series 3 _____

When the assignment is complete, close the file without saving it again.

TICKLERS (optional)

Worksheet. The problem thus far has assumed that assets are depreciated a full year in the year acquired. Normally, depreciation begins in the month acquired. For example, an asset acquired at the beginning of April is depreciated for only nine months in the year of acquisition. Modify the DEPREC3 worksheet to include the month of acquisition as an additional item of input. To demonstrate proper handling of this factor on the depreciation schedule, modify the formulas for the first two years. Some of the formulas may not actually need to be revised. Do not modify the formulas for Years 3 through 8 and ignore the numbers shown in those years. Some will be incorrect as will be some of the totals. Use the Print Preview command (File menu) to make sure that the worksheet will print neatly on one page, then print the worksheet. Save the completed file as DEPRECT.

Hint: Insert the month in row 6 of the Data Section specifying the month by a number (e.g., April is the fourth month of the year). Redo the formulas in rows 29 and 30. For the units of production method, assume no change in the estimated hours for both years.

Chart. Using the DEPREC6 file, prepare a line chart or XY chart that plots annual depreciation expense under all three depreciation methods. No chart data table is needed; use the range B29 to E36 on the Worksheet as a basis for preparing the chart if you prepare an XY chart. Use C29 to E36 if you prepare a line chart. Put your name somewhere on the chart. Save the file again as DEPREC6. Print the chart.

	A	B	C	D	E
1					
2			*DEPREC*		
3			Depreciation		
4					
5		Data Section			
6					
7		Cost of asset		$266,000	
8		Estimated salvage value		$26,000	
9		Estimated useful life in years		4	
10		Estimated life in units (miles, etc.)*		100,000	
11					
12			*Estimated		
13		Year	Units		
14		1	20,000		
15		2	30,000		
16		3	40,000		
17		4	10,000		
18		5	0		
19		6	0		
20		7	0		
21		8	0		
22					
23		Answer Section			
24					
25			Depreciation Expense		
26					Double
27			Straight	Units of	Declining
28		Year	Line	Production	Balance
29		1	FORMULA1	FORMULA5	FORMULA9
30		2	FORMALA2	FORMULA6	FORMULA10
31		3	FORMALA3	FORMULA7	FORMULA11
32		4	FORMULA4	FORMALA8	FORMULA12
33		5	0	0	0
34		6	0	0	0
35		7	0	0	0
36		8	0	0	0
37		Total	$0	$0	$0
38					

P10 ◆ PAYROLL REGISTER (PR)

LEARNING OBJECTIVES

- Prepare and use a payroll register including Social Security and Medicare withholdings.
- Use =IF and =ROUND to design the Social Security tax and union dues formulas.
- Record journal entries for payroll, employer's tax liability, and payment of payroll taxes.
- Identify behavior patterns among payroll taxes over time.
- Alter the worksheet to include an additional employee.
- Create a chart showing the percentage of an employee's gross pay that is withheld for taxes, etc., and how much is left over as net pay.

PROBLEM DATA

Design World has five employees, and they are paid at the end of each month. Payroll data for November are as follows:

Employee	Gross Pay for November	Federal Income Tax Withheld	Cumulative Gross Pay to October 31
Anders	$9,000	$2,500	$?
Brayer	1,530	302	15,570
Jacobs	1,210	266	6,550
Malone	8,837	2,385	99,500
Wilson	4,200	1,355	55,000

Other information (using 2003 rates) is as follows:

a. Social Security taxes are 6.2% on monthly gross pay up to a cumulative total pay of $87,000 for each employee per year.
b. Medicare taxes are 1.45% on monthly gross pay with no upper limit.
c. A $25 monthly deduction is made for union dues for all union members.
d. Unemployment taxes are paid on monthly gross pay up to the first $7,000 earned by each employee each year. State and federal rates are 2.7% and 0.8% respectively.

REQUIRED

1. Based on 2003 tax rates provided, use a calculator to compute how much would be withheld from Anders' November paycheck in the following three cases (round to the nearest penny):

Cumulative Gross Pay to October 31	Social Security	Medicare
$70,000	_____	_____
$85,000	_____	_____
$100,000	_____	_____

2. You have been asked to record the November payroll information using a payroll register and a general journal. Review the printout of the worksheet PR, a computerized payroll register, that follows these requirements. The columns will automatically retotal as new entries are made. Entries in column B indicate whether or not employees are union members. Assume Anders cumulative gross pay to October 31 could be $70,000, or $85,000, or $100,000.

3. To make the worksheet reusable each month, the Social Security tax formulas should be designed to automatically compute whether 1) full tax is due, 2) no tax is due (e.g., cumulative gross pay is over the ceiling), or 3) some tax is due. =IF statements will be required. Also, the =ROUND function should be used for Formulas 1 through 3 to eliminate rounding errors. FORMULA2 has been provided for you below. Review Appendix A of *Excel Quick* and explain the meaning of each part of the formula.

| ——(a) ——|—— (b) ——|—————— (c) —————————|—— (d)——|(e)|

FORMULA2:   =ROUND(IF(I14>G25,0,IF((I14+C14)>G25,(G25-I14)*G23,C14*G23)),2)

a.

b.

c.

d.

e.

4. In the spaces provided below, write the other formulas requested. FORMULA4 should also use the =IF function.

    FORMULA1_____

    FORMULA3_____

    FORMULA4_____

    FORMULA5_____

5. Start the spreadsheet program and open the file PR from the student disk. Enter the gross pay and federal income tax withheld for each employee and enter $70,000 for Anders cumulative gross pay (cell I13). Then, enter the formulas where indicated on the worksheet. As the formulas are entered, the cells that contain zeros will be automatically filled. Enter your name in cell A1. Save the completed file as PR5. Print the worksheet when done. Also print your formulas. *Check figure: Anders' net pay (cell H13), $5,786.50.*

WHAT-IF ANALYSIS

6. Verify that your formulas for Anders work by entering $85,000 and $100,000 for cumulative gross pay in cell I13. Compare your withholding amounts to your answers in requirement 1 above. Correct your formulas if necessary and save the file as PR5 again.

7. In the space provided below, prepare the journal entry to record the November payroll for *all* employees assuming that the payroll is paid on November 30 and that Anders cumulative gross pay (cell I13) is $70,000.

8. In the space provided below, prepare the journal entry as of November 30 to record the employer's payroll taxes for November. Also prepare the journal entries to record the payment of all payroll taxes and union dues, assuming that they are all due on December 15.

9. **Optional:** Revise the data in rows 22–25 using updated tax information for your current year. This will be provided by your instructor. Save the revised file as PR9. Print the worksheet when done.

CHART ANALYSIS

10. Click the Chart sheet tab. On the screen is a chart of the four payroll taxes that Design World incurs in total during the year. By the behaviors shown on the chart, identify below which of the four taxes each represents.

A _____

B _____

C _____

D _____

When the assignment is complete, close the file without saving it again.

TICKLERS (optional)

Worksheet. A new employee was hired during November and was mistakenly omitted from the payroll register. The employee's last name is Yeoman, and the gross pay for November is $1,300. Add the new employee to the PR5 worksheet and include all standard withholding rates in computing net pay. Federal income tax withheld is $175. He is a union member. Use the Print Preview command (File menu) to make sure that the worksheet will print neatly on one page, then print the worksheet. Save the completed file as PRT.

Chart. Using the PR5 file, prepare a 3D pie chart to show the percentage of an employee's gross pay that is withheld for taxes, Social Security, etc., and how much is left over as net pay. Use Jacobs as your example. Complete the Chart Tickler Data Table and use it as a basis for preparing the chart. Put your name somewhere on the chart. Save the file again as PR5. Print the chart.

	A	B	C	D	E	F	G	H	I
2					*PR*				
3					*Payroll Register*				
4									
5					Design World				
6					Payroll Register				
7					November				
8									
9					Deductions				
10				Federal	Social				Cum.
11			Gross	Income	Security	Medicare	Union		Gross Pay
12	Employee	U	Pay	Tax	Tax	Tax	Dues	Net Pay	to Oct 31
13	Anders	Y			FORM1	FORM3	FORM4	FORM5	?
14	Brayer	N			FORM2	0.00	0.00	0.00	15,570
15	Jacobs	Y			0.00	0.00	0.00	0.00	6,550
16	Malone	N			0.00	0.00	0.00	0.00	99,500
17	Wilson	N			0.00	0.00	0.00	0.00	55,000
18			0.00	0.00	0.00	0.00	0.00	0.00	
19									
20									
21					Tax Information				
22					Current Year		2003		
23					FICA tax rate		6.20%		
24					Medicare tax rate		1.45%		
25					FICA tax maximum income		$87,000		
26									

P11 ♦ BOND PRICING AND AMORTIZATION (BONDS)

LEARNING OBJECTIVES

- Calculate bond issuance prices (with detailed assistance) and develop amortization schedules. Record entries for bond issuance and interest expense using both the straight-line and effective interest method of amortization.
- Calculate bond prices after issuance.
- Interpret the relationship between bond prices and years to maturity.
- Alter the worksheet to accommodate bonds with up to 20 years maturity.
- Create a chart plotting the annual interest expense under both the straight-line and effective interest methods.

PROBLEM DATA

Universal Enterprises recently issued $1,000,000 of 10-year, 8% bonds at an effective interest rate of 9%. Bond interest is payable annually.

REQUIRED

1. You have been asked to calculate the issuance price of the bonds and prepare amortization schedules for any discount or premium. The worksheet BONDS has been provided to assist you. Note that the worksheet contains a Scratch Pad at the bottom that has been pre-programmed to automatically compute and display the relevant cash flows needed for bond pricing.

2. The bond pricing formula utilizes the Net Present Value function on your spreadsheet program. The formula is broken into two parts as identified by the letters in parentheses above the formula. See Appendix A in *Excel Quick* for a discussion on the NPV function, and then explain the meaning of each part of the formula.

    |——— (a) ———|——— (b) ———|

    FORMULA1:   =NPV(E10,C60:C71)+NPV(E10,D60:D71)

    a.

    b.

3. Using the spaces provided, write the formulas required to complete the worksheet. Assume all bonds have at least a two-year maturity. Year 0 is the date of issuance. Bond discount (column E) should be a negative number, and bond premium should be a positive number. The amortization of bond discount (column C in the straight-line table and column D in the effective interest table) should be a positive number, and the amortization of bond premium should be a negative number.

FORMULA2_____   FORMULA14_____

FORMULA3_____   FORMULA15_____

FORMULA4_____   FORMULA16_____

FORMULA5_____   FORMULA17_____

FORMULA6_____   FORMULA18_____

FORMULA7_____   FORMULA19_____

FORMULA8_____   FORMULA20_____

FORMULA9_____   FORMULA21_____

FORMULA10_____   FORMULA22_____

FORMULA11_____   FORMULA23_____

FORMULA12_____   FORMULA24_____

FORMULA13_____   FORMULA25_____

4. Start the spreadsheet program and open the file BONDS from the file disk. Enter the formulas in the appropriate cells. Enter your name in cell A1. Save the file as BONDS4. Print the worksheet when done. *Check figures: Bond issue price (cell F17), $935,823; Bond carrying value for Year 10 (cells F32 and F49), $ 1,000,000.*

5. Prepare journal entries in the space provided below to record (a) the issuance of the bond, (b) the interest payment and required amortization for Year 1 using the straight-line method of amortization, and (c) the interest payment and required amortization for Year 1 using the effective interest method of amortization.

WHAT-IF ANALYSIS

6.   Use the worksheet to compute the bond issue price and amortization schedules if the effective interest rate is 7%. Save the file as BONDS6. Print the worksheet when done. Also, repeat Requirement 5 in the space provided below for this bond.

7.   Use the worksheet to compute the bond issue price if the effective interest rate is 8%.

    Bond issue price $_____

8.   Find the effective interest rate for $5,000,000 of 6-year, 8% bonds (interest payable annually) which were issued for $5,189,490. To do this, enter the known information in the Data Section and experiment with different effective interest rates until you get a bond price of exactly $5,189,490. (You may have to use an effective interest rate with decimals.) Print the worksheet when done.

CHART ANALYSIS

9.   a.   Reset the Data Section to its initial values. The price of this bond is $935,823. What would it be if there were only 9 or 8 years to maturity? Use the worksheet to compute the bond issue prices and enter them below.

        Bond issue price (9 years to maturity) $_____
        Bond issue price (8 years to maturity) $_____

    b.   Compare these prices to the bond-carrying values found in the effective interest amortization schedule you originally printed out in Requirement 4. Explain the similarity.
    c.   Click the Chart sheet tab. The chart presented shows the price behavior of this bond based on years to maturity. Explain what effect years to maturity has on bond prices. Check your explanation by trying 7% as the effective rate (cell E10) and clicking the Chart sheet tab again. Also try 8%.

When the assignment is complete, close the file without saving it again.

TICKLERS (optional)

Worksheet. Modify the BONDS4 worksheet to accommodate bonds with up to 20-year maturities. Use your new model to determine the issue price and amortization schedules of a $2,000,000, 18-year, 9% bond issued to yield 10%. Use the Print Preview command (File menu) to make sure that the worksheet will print neatly, then print the worksheet. Save the completed file as BONDST.

Hint: Expand both amortization schedules to 20 years. Expand the Scratch Pad to 20 years. Modify FORMULA1 in cell F17 to include the new ranges.

Chart. Using the BONDS4 file, prepare a line chart that plots annual interest expense over the ten- year life of this bond under both the straight-line and effective interest methods. No chart data table is needed. Put A23 to A32 in the Label format and then select A23 to A32, D23 to D32, and B40 to B49 as a collection. Enter all appropriate titles, legends, formats, and so forth. Put your name somewhere on the chart. Save the file again as BONDS4. Print the chart.

		A	B	C	D	E	F
2				BONDS			
3				Bond Pricing and Amortization			
4							
5		Data Section					
6							
7			Face value of bond			$1,000,000	
8			Years to maturity *			10	
9			Stated interest rate			8.0%	
10			Effective interest rate			9.0%	
11							
12			* Worksheet is designed for use with bonds having a maturity of				
13			12 years or less and paying interest annually.				
14							
15		Answer Section					
16							
17			Bond issue price				FORMULA1
18							
19				Amortization Schedule - Straight Line Method			
20			Cash		Interest	(Disc.)	Bond
21		Year	Paid	Amortization	Expense	Premium	Carrying Value
22		0				FORMULA2	FORMULA3
23		1	FORMULA4	FORMULA5	FORMULA6	FORMULA7	FORMULA8
24		2	FORMULA9	FORMULA10	FORMULA11	FORMULA12	FORMULA13
25		3	0	0	0	0	0
26		4	0	0	0	0	0
27		5	0	0	0	0	0
28		6	0	0	0	0	0
29		7	0	0	0	0	0
30		8	0	0	0	0	0
31		9	0	0	0	0	0
32		10	0	0	0	0	0
33		11	0	0	0	0	0
34		12	0	0	0	0	0
35							
36				Amortization Schedule - Effective Interest Method			
37			Interest	Cash		(Disc.)	Bond
38		Year	Expense	Paid	Amortization	Premium	Carrying Value
39		0				FORMULA14	FORMULA15
40		1	FORMULA16	FORMULA17	FORMULA18	FORMULA19	FORMULA20
41		2	FORMULA21	FORMULA22	FORMULA23	FORMULA24	FORMULA25
42		3	0	0	0	0	0
43		4	0	0	0	0	0
44		5	0	0	0	0	0
45		6	0	0	0	0	0
46		7	0	0	0	0	0
47		8	0	0	0	0	0
48		9	0	0	0	0	0
49		10	0	0	0	0	0
50		11	0	0	0	0	0
51		12	0	0	0	0	0
52							

	B	C	D
56	Scratch Pad		
57	Display of relevant cash flows		
58		Annual	Bond
59	Year	Interest	Maturity
60	1	80000	0
61	2	80000	0
62	3	80000	0
63	4	80000	0
64	5	80000	0
65	6	80000	0
66	7	80000	0
67	8	80000	0
68	9	80000	0
69	10	80000	1000000
70	11	0	0
71	12	0	0

P12 ◆ STATEMENT OF STOCKHOLDERS' EQUITY (STOCKEQ)

LEARNING OBJECTIVES

- Analyze equity transactions and prepare statements of stockholders' equity.
- Prepare the stockholders' equity section of the balance sheet.
- Alter the worksheet to include additional stockholders' equity accounts.
- Create a column chart showing year-end stockholders' equity account balances.

PROBLEM DATA

Huckleberry Corporation began 2003 with these stockholders' equity balances:

Preferred stock, $100 par value, 8% cumulative	$ 5,000
Common stock, $2 par value	40,000
Additional paid-in capital	27,000
Retained earnings	83,000
Less: Treasury stock (3,300 shares at cost)	(13,200)
Total stockholders' equity	$141,800

The following selected transactions and events occurred during the year:

a.   Issued 5,000 shares of common stock for $30,000.
b.   Purchased 600 shares of treasury stock for $2,400.
c.   Sold 1,000 shares of treasury stock for $5,500.
d.   Generated net income of $47,000.
e.   Declared and paid the full year's dividend on preferred stock and a dividend of $1.00 per share on common stock outstanding at the end of the year.

Huckleberry maintains several paid-in capital accounts (Excess of Par, Treasury Stock, etc.) in its ledger, but combines them all as "Additional paid-in capital" when preparing financial statements.

REQUIRED

1.   You have been asked to prepare a statement of stockholders' equity for Huckleberry Corporation. Review the worksheet STOCKEQ that follows these requirements.

2.   Using the spaces provided below, write the two formulas required to complete the worksheet.

FORMULA1 _____

FORMULA2 _____

3. Start the spreadsheet program and open the file STOCKEQ from the Student Disk. Enter the formulas in the appropriate cells on the worksheet. Then fill in the columns to show the effect of each of the selected transactions and events listed above. Enter your name in cell A1. Save the completed worksheet as STOCKEQ3. Print the worksheet. Also print your formulas. *Check figure: Total stockholders' equity balance at 12/31/03, $199,400.*

4. In the space provided below, prepare the stockholders' equity section of Huckleberry Corporation's balance sheet as of December 31, 2003. Use proper headings and provide full disclosure of all appropriate information. Huckleberry's corporate charter authorizes the issuance of 1,000 shares of preferred stock and 100,000 shares of common stock.

WHAT-IF ANALYSIS

5. The following selected transactions and events occurred during 2004:

   a. Issued 100 shares of preferred stock for $10,000.
   b. Sold 400 shares of treasury stock for $1,400.
   c. Declared and issued a 4% common stock dividend. The market value on the date of declaration was $5 per share.
   d. Generated a net loss for the year of $8,000.
   e. Declared and paid the full year's dividend on all the preferred stock and a dividend of $.15 per share on common stock outstanding at the end of the year.

   Enter beginning balances for 2004 on STOCKEQ3. Then erase all 2003 entries and enter the above transactions for 2004. Save the results as STOCKEQ5. Print the results.

CHART ANALYSIS

6. Click the Chart sheet tab. The stacked bar chart shows Huckleberry's equity account balance at December 31, 2004. Match the stacked bars (A–G) that best describe what will happen to the equity accounts if the following transactions and events occur in 2005. Letters may be repeated or not used. Consider each case independently.

		Stacked Bar Letter
a.	Reports net income	_____
b.	Declares cash dividend	_____
c.	Issues additional stock	_____
d.	Retires stock	_____
e.	Splits stock 3 for 2	_____
f.	Pays cash dividend	_____
g.	Declares stock dividend	_____

When the assignment is complete, close the file without saving it again.

TICKLERS (optional)

Worksheet. Suppose that the $27,000 "Additional paid-in capital" balance at December 31, 2002, comes from two ledger accounts: $21,000 from Paid-in capital in excess of par and $6,000 from Paid-in capital from treasury stock transactions. Revise the STOCKEQ3 worksheet to show a column for each of these accounts instead of the single column for Additional paid-in capital. Then redo the 2003 transactions using the new columns. Use the Print Preview command to make sure that the worksheet will print neatly on one page, then print the worksheet. Save the file as STOCKEQT.

Chart. Using the STOCKEQ5 file, prepare a column chart showing the dollar amount of each of the stockholders' equity account balances at December 31, 2004. Treasury stock can be shown as a negative value. Put your name somewhere on the chart. Save the file again as STOCKEQ5. Print the chart.

	A	B	C	D	E	F	G
2	STOCKEQ						
3	Statement of Stockholder's Equity						
4							
5			Huckleberry Corporation				
6			Statement of Stockholders' Equity				
7			For the Year Ended December 31, 2003				
8							
9		Preferred	Common				
10		Stock	Stock	Add'l			
11		$100 Par	$2 Par	Paid-in	Retained	Treasury	
12		Value	Value	Capital	Earnings	Stock	Total
13	Balance, 12	$5,000	$40,000	$27,000	$83,000	($13,200)	$141,800
14	Common stock issued						FORMUL2
15	Treasury stock bought						0
16	Treasury stock sold						0
17	Net income						0
18	Dividends declared:						
19	Preferred						0
20	Common						0
21	Balance, 12	FORMUL1	$40,000	$27,000	$83,000	($13,200)	$141,800
22							

P13 ♦ EARNINGS PER SHARE (EPS)

LEARNING OBJECTIVES

- Compute basic and diluted earnings per share for a company that:
  - (1) issues additional common stock during the year
  - (2) has convertible preferred stock outstanding
  - (3) has discontinued operations
- Contrast trends in income from continuing operations and net income using both total dollars and earnings per share.
- Alter the worksheet to include a change in accounting principle.
- Create a column chart plotting shares outstanding over time.

PROBLEM DATA

Seasons, Inc. had 50,000 shares of common stock and 10,000 shares of $100 par value, 8% preferred stock outstanding on January 1, 2004. Each share of preferred stock is convertible into four shares of common stock. The stock has not been converted. During the year, Seasons issued additional shares of common stock as follows:

April 1	10,000 shares
August 1	30,000 shares
October 1	10,000 shares

For 2004, Seasons, Inc. had income from continuing operations of $515,000 and a $90,000 loss from discontinued operations (net of tax).

REQUIRED

1. As vice president of finance for the store, you have been asked to calculate earnings per share for 2004. The worksheet EPS has been provided to assist you.

2. In the spaces provided below, enter the seven formulas needed to complete the worksheet.

FORMULA1_____   FORMULA5_____

FORMULA2_____   FORMULA6_____

FORMULA3_____   FORMULA7_____

FORMULA4_____

3. Start the spreadsheet program and open the file EPS from the Student Disk. Enter all input items (A–F) in the appropriate cells in the Data Section. Enter all formulas in the appropriate cells in the Answer Section. Enter your name in cell A1. Save the completed file as EPS3. Print the worksheet when done. Also print your formulas. *Check figure: Primary earnings per share from continuing operations (cell D29), $6.00.*

WHAT-IF ANALYSIS

4. During 2005, Seasons issued 24,000 additional shares of common stock on June 1 and 30,000 on November 1. The company earned $603,000 from continuing operations and $28,000 from another segment of the business that was discontinued during the year. Use your completed worksheet to prepare a computation of earnings per share for 2005. Erase any data in the Data Section that is not required for 2005. Save the solution for 2005 as EPS4 and print the results.

CHART ANALYSIS

5. Open the EPS4 file. You are going to compare two charts in this step. To begin, click the Total Income sheet tab. The chart that appears on the screen depicts the trend for income from continuing operations and net income. Rather impressive improvement!

Now click the Basic EPS sheet tab. This chart shows the trend for primary earnings per share. Rather dismal!

Given the impressive results in the first chart and the disappointing trends in the second chart, should the stockholders be pleased or unhappy? Explain.

When the assignment is complete, close the file without saving it again.

TICKLERS (optional)

Worksheet. Open the EPS4 file. Suppose that Seasons had also changed its inventory valuation method from FIFO to weighted-average during 2005. A review of the accounting records reveals that total after-tax income would have been $52,000 less had the weighted-average method been employed in earlier years. Revise the worksheet to accommodate this new item and recompute earnings per share. Use the Print Preview command (File menu) to make sure that the worksheet will print neatly on one page, then print the worksheet. Save the completed file as EPST.

Chart. Using the EPS3 file, create a column chart that plots the total number of common shares outstanding on a month-by-month basis throughout 2004. Complete the Chart Tickler Data Table (beginning on row 42 of the Total Income sheet tab) and use it as a basis for preparing the chart. Enter all appropriate titles, legends, and formats. Put your name somewhere on the chart. Save the chart again as EPS3. Print the chart.

	A	B	C	D	E	F
2			*EPS*			
3			*Earnings Per Share*			
4						
5	Data Section					
6						
7	Year		2004			
8						
9	Preferred stock		8%			
10		$100	par			
11		10,000	shares outstanding		12	months
12			4 conversion rate into common stock			
13						
14	Common stock	$10	par			
15		50,000	shares outstanding		3	months
16		Input A	shares outstanding		Input B	months
17		Input C	shares outstanding		Input D	months
18		Input E	shares outstanding		Input F	months
19						
20	Net income	$515,000	from continuing operations			
21		(90,000)	from discontinued segment (net of tax)			
22						
23	Answer Section					
24						
25	Weighted average common shares outstanding			FORMULA1		
26						
27						
28	Earnings (loss) per common share			Basic	Diluted	
29	Continuing operations			FORMULA2	FORMULA5	
30	Discontinued operations			FORMULA3	FORMULA6	
31	Net income			FORMULA4	FORMULA7	
32						

P14 ♦ STATEMENT OF CASH FLOWS (CASHFLOW)

LEARNING OBJECTIVES

- Prepare a worksheet for the statement of cash flows.
- Prepare a statement of cash flows.
- Interpret cash flow trends from operating, investing, and financing activities.
- Alter the worksheet to include a statement of cash flows.
- Create a chart illustrating the historical relationship between operating cash flows and net income.

PROBLEM DATA

The comparative balance sheet of Creative Concepts Corporation at June 30, the end of the fiscal year, is as follows:

Creative Concepts Corporation
Comparative Balance Sheet
June 30, 2005 and 2004

Assets	2005	2004
Cash	$ 57,210	$ 39,600
Accounts receivable	131,250	112,215
Merchandise inventory	200,100	210,930
Prepaid expenses	10,350	10,875
Plant assets	460,500	315,000
Accumulated depreciation—plant assets	(128,550)	(90,000)
Total assets	$730,860	$598,620
Liabilities & Stockholders' Equity		
Accounts payable	$ 61,110	$ 59,220
Dividends payable	54,000	30,000
Bonds payable	120,000	105,000
Common stock, $20 par	240,000	210,000
Premium on common stock	33,000	22,500
Retained earnings	222,750	171,900
Total liabilities & stockholders' equity	$730,860	$598,620

Additional data obtained from the records of Creative Concepts Corporation are as follows:

a. Net income for fiscal 2005 was $104,850.
b. Depreciation reported on income statement for fiscal 2005 was $46,500.

c. Purchased $165,000 of new equipment, putting $90,000 cash down and issuing $75,000 of bonds for the balance.

d. Old equipment originally costing $19,500, with accumulated depreciation of $7,950, was sold for $13,500.

e. Retired $60,000 of bonds.

f. Declared cash dividends of $54,000.

g. Issued 1,500 shares of common stock at $27 cash.

REQUIRED

1. You have been asked to prepare a statement of cash flows for Creative Concepts Corporation. Review the worksheet called CASHFLOW that has been provided to assist you in preparing the statement. The worksheet has been designed so that as you make entries in columns D and F, column G will be automatically updated. Columns C and E are to be used to enter letter references for each of the debit and credit entries on the worksheet.

2. Using the spaces provided below, write the formulas requested in the worksheet. FORMULA1 has been provided for you as an example.

FORMULA1 __=B17+D17-F17__   FORMULA4 _____

FORMULA2 _____   FORMULA5 _____

FORMULA3 _____   FORMULA6 _____

3. Start the spreadsheet program and open the file CASHFLOW from the file disk. First, enter the formulas. Then, complete the worksheet in the manner described below:

According to the problem, cash increased from $39,600 to $57,210 during the year. This is a $17,610 increase. To record this increase on the worksheet, move to row 17. Since this is the first account you are analyzing, enter the letter **a** in column C. Then enter **17610** in column D (a debit since cash increased). This brings the year-end balance (column G) to $57,210, its proper balance.

Now move to the bottom part of the statement where you see the categories Operating Activities, Investing Activities, etc. The credit side of the entry has to be entered here.

The proper space for this cash entry is on row 58. Enter the letter **a** in cell E58 and **17610** in cell F58. Notice the totals at the bottom of the page (row 59) now agree.

The next account balance that changed is accounts receivable. It increased by $19,035. To enter this change on the worksheet, enter the letter **b** in cell C18 and **19035** in cell D18 (again a debit since accounts receivable increased). This brings the year-end balance in column G to $131,250, its proper balance. The change in accounts receivable balance is an operating activity adjustment (as explained in your textbook). Enter the credit side of this entry in cells E34 and F34, and enter the explanation **Increase in accounts receivable** in cell A34. *Note:* Your textbook probably shows "Net income" as the first item under Operating Activities. We will get to that later. The sequence that you enter items on this worksheet is not important.

All other balance sheet accounts must be analyzed in the same manner, placing appropriate debit or credit entries in the top part of the worksheet to obtain the proper balances in column G, and then entering the second side of the entry in the appropriate row on the bottom part of the worksheet. You should use letter references to identify all entries. Also, you must enter a description of the entry in column A under the appropriate activity category. Although a sequence of analyzing the balance sheet from top to bottom is suggested here, this order is not necessary. As mentioned above, your textbook may specify a different sequence. Also, note that some accounts may have both debit and credit adjustments to them.

The worksheet is not a substitute for a statement of cash flows, but it does provide you with all the numbers you need to properly prepare one.

You will be done with your analysis when:

a. The individual account balances at June 30, 2005, as shown on the worksheet (column G) equal those shown in the problem data above.

b. The transaction column totals are equal (cells D59 and F59).

When you are finished, enter your name in cell A1. Save your completed file as CASHFLO3. Print the worksheet when done. Also print your formulas. *Check figure: Total credits at 6/30/2005 (cell G31) $859,410.*

4. In the space provided on the next page, prepare a statement of cash flows in good form using the indirect method. Use the format shown in your textbook.

WHAT-IF ANALYSIS

5. Suppose that an audit of Creative Concepts Corporation encountered the following two errors:

a. An accounts receivable totaling $4,500 should have been written off as a bad debt at the end of the year. Year-end accounts receivable should be only $126,750.

b. The $54,000 dividend declared at year-end had in fact been paid. Thus, both the cash account and the dividends payable account are overstated at year-end.

Correct both errors on the worksheet. Save your completed file as CASHFLO5. Print the worksheet when done.

Creative Concepts Corporation
Statement of Cash Flows
For the Year Ended June 30, 2005

CHART ANALYSIS

6. Click the Chart sheet tab. On the chart, the components of cash flow for Creative Concepts Corporation over the last five years are plotted. Comment below on the behavior of each component. Do you see favorable trends? Unfavorable ones?

When the assignment is complete, close the file without saving it again.

TICKLERS (optional)

Worksheet. Place a formal statement of cash flows (see Requirement 4 above) on the CASH-FLO3 worksheet. Use columns I through O for your statement. Put your name at the top. Print your work (select and print just the statement of cash flow cells). Use the Print Preview command (File menu) to make sure that the statement (not the worksheet) will print neatly on one page, then print it out. Save the completed file as CASHFLOT.

Chart. Using the CASH3 file, prepare a line chart that illustrates the relationship between operating cash flows and net income over the last five years. Use the appropriate columns on the Chart Data Table as a basis for preparing the chart. Use all appropriate titles, legends, formatting, etc. Put your name somewhere on the chart. Save the file again as CASHFLO3. Print the chart.

	A	B	C	D	E	F	G
2		CASHFLOW					
3		Statement of Cash Flows					
4							
5		Creative Concepts Corporation					
6		Work Sheet for Statement of Cash Flows					
7		For Year Ended June 30, 2005					
8							
9							
10				Analysis of			
11				Transactions for			
12				Year Ended 6/30/05			
13		Account					Account
14		Balance					Balance
15		6/30/04		Debit		Credit	6/30/05
16	Debits						
17	Cash	39,600					FORMULA1
18	Accounts receivable	112,215					FORMULA2
19	Merchandise inventory	210,930					FORMULA3
20	Prepaid expenses	10,875					0
21	Plant assets	315,000					0
22	Total	688,620					0
23	Credits						
24	Accumulated depreciation	90,000					FORMULA4
25	Accounts payable	59,220					FORMULA5
26	Dividends payable	30,000					FORMULA6
27	Bonds payable	105,000					0
28	Common stock, $20 par	210,000					0
29	Premium on common stock	22,500					0
30	Retained earnings	171,900					0
31	Total	688,620					0
32							

	A	B	C	D	E	F	G
33	Operating Activities						
34							
35							
36							
37							
38							
39							
40							
41							
42							
43	Investing Activities						
44							
45							
46							
47							
48	Financing Activities						
49							
50							
51							
52							
53							
54	Noncash Investing & Financing						
55							
56							
57					0		0	
58	Change in cash						
59					0		0	
60							

P15 ♦ RATIO ANALYSIS (RATIOA)

LEARNING OBJECTIVES

- Using ten key ratios, perform standard analysis on a company over a three-year period.
- Interpret the results and compare them to industry norms.
- Contrast rate of return on assets with rate of return on equity.
- Alter the worksheet to include two additional ratios.
- Create a chart contrasting the quick (acid test) and current ratios.

PROBLEM DATA

The comparative financial statements of Global Technology are as follows:

Global Technology
Comparative Income Statement
For Years Ended December 31, 2004 and 2003

	2004	2003
Net sales	$ 3,516,075	$ 3,300,330
Cost of merchandise sold	2,820,000	2,550,000
Gross profit	$ 696,075	$ 750,330
Selling expenses	$ 123,000	$ 127,500
General expenses	81,660	88,500
Total operating expenses	$ 204,660	$ 216,000
Operating income	$ 491,415	$ 534,330
Other expense (interest)	36,000	19,500
Income before income tax	$ 455,415	$ 514,830
Income tax	164,400	220,905
Net income	$ 291,015	$ 293,925

Global Technology
Comparative Retained Earnings Statement
For Years Ended December 31, 2004 and 2003

	2004	2003
Retained earnings, January 1	$ 1,420,095	$ 1,186,170
Net income for year	291,015	293,925
Total	$ 1,711,110	$ 1,480,095
Common stock dividends	82,500	60,000
Retained earnings, December 31	$ 1,628,610	$ 1,420,095

Global Technology
Comparative Balance Sheet
December 31, 2004 and 2003

Assets	2004	2003
Cash	$ 34,830	$ 63,000
Accounts receivable	232,500	298,575
Merchandise inventory	825,480	637,500
Prepaid expenses	22,500	25,500
Plant assets (net)	1,800,000	1,530,000
Total assets	$2,915,310	$2,554,575

Liabilities & Stockholders' Equity	2004	2003
Accounts payable	$ 326,400	$ 339,180
Bonds payable, 10% due 2010	360,000	195,000
Total liabilities	$ 686,400	$ 534,180
Common stock	$ 600,300	$ 600,300
Retained earnings	1,628,610	1,420,095
Total stockholders' equity	$2,228,910	$2,020,395
Total liabilities & stockholders' equity	$2,915,310	$2,554,575

REQUIRED

1. Review the worksheet RATIOA that follows these requirements. You have been asked to perform a ratio analysis of this company for 2004.

2. In the spaces provided below, write the formulas requested.

FORMULA1_____   FORMULA6_____

FORMULA2_____   FORMULA7_____

FORMULA3_____   FORMULA8_____

FORMULA4_____   FORMULA9_____

FORMULA5_____   FORMULA10_____

3. Start the spreadsheet program and open the file RATIOA from the Student Disk. Enter the formulas in the appropriate cells. Enter your name in cell A1. Save the completed model as RATIOA3. Print the worksheet when done. Also print your formulas. *Check figure: Acid test (quick) ratio (cell C58), .82.*

4. a. What information does a comparison of the current ratio and acid test ratio provide?

    b. Is the company using leverage to its advantage? Explain.

    c. What other observations can be made comparing Global Technology's ratios to the following industry norms:

Acid test ratio	1.0
Current ratio	2.0
Accounts receivable turnover	12.0
Inventory turnover	4.0
Gross profit ratio	40%
Net income to sales	7%
Rate earned on total assets	12%
Rate earned on common stock equity	20%
Debt to total assets	.35
Times interest earned	8

WHAT-IF ANALYSIS

5. Prepare a ratio analysis for Global Technology for 2005. The following information is available for 2005:

Accounts payable	$ 342,240	Income tax	$ 135,300
Accounts receivable	206,400	Merchandise inventory	814,500
Bonds payable	360,000	Net sales	3,753,000
Cash	?	Other expenses (interest)	36,000
Common stock	600,300	Plant assets	2,025,000
Common stock dividends	102,000	Prepaid expenses	4,500
Cost of goods sold	3,102,000	Selling expenses	132,000
General expenses	84,750		

The 2005 information should be entered in column B of the RATIOA3 worksheet. The 2004 information should be entered in column C. Save the revised file as RATIOA5. Print the worksheet when done.

111

6. Compare your printout from requirement 3 with your printout from requirement 5. From these two sets of ratios, what conclusions can be drawn concerning changes from 2004 and 2005?

CHART ANALYSIS

7. With the 2005 data still on the screen, click the Chart sheet tab. The chart presented shows the rates of return for Global Technology for the last five years. Answer the following questions:

   a. In 2001, the rate of return on assets exceeded the rate of return on common stockholders' equity. Why might this have occurred? Be as specific as possible.

   b. Is the company better off in 2005 than it was in 2001? Why or why not?

   When the assignment is complete, close the file without saving it again.

TICKLERS (optional)

Worksheet. Modify the RATIOA5 worksheet to have it compute two additional activity ratios: number of days' sales in receivables and number of days' sales in merchandise inventory. Use the 2004 and 2005 data and assume a 365-day year. Write out the formulas for your ratios below.

Days' sales in receivables_____

Days' sales in inventory _____

Use the Print Preview command (File menu) to make sure that the worksheet will print neatly, then print the worksheet. Save the completed file as RATIOAT.

Chart. Using the RATIOA5 file, prepare a column chart that compares the acid test and current ratios for Global Technology for 2004 and 2005. Complete the Chart Tickler Data Table and use it as a basis for preparing the chart. Enter all appropriate titles, legends, and formats. Put your name somewhere on the chart. Save the file again as RATIOA5. Print the chart.

	A	B	C
2	**RATIOA**		
3	Ratio Analysis		
4			
5	Data Section		
6			
7	Global Technology		
8	Comparative Income Statement		
9	For Years Ended December 31, 2004 and 2003		
10		2004	2003
11	Net sales	$3,516,075	$3,300,330
12	Cost of merchandise sold	2,820,000	2,550,000
13	Gross profit	$696,075	$750,330
14	Selling expenses	$123,000	$127,500
15	General expenses	81,660	88,500
16	Total operating expenses	$204,660	$216,000
17	Operating income	$491,415	$534,330
18	Other expenses (interest)	36,000	19,500
19	Income before income tax	$455,415	$514,830
20	Income tax	164,400	220,905
21	Net income	$291,015	$293,925
22			
23			
24	Global Technology		
25	Comparative Retained Earnings Statement		
26	For Years Ended December 31, 2004 and 2003		
27		2004	2003
28	Retained earnings, January 1	$1,420,095	$1,186,170
29	Net income for year	291,015	293,925
30	Total	$1,711,110	$1,480,095
31	Common stock dividends	82,500	60,000
32	Retained earnings, December 31	$1,628,610	$1,420,095
33			
34			
35	Global Technology		
36	Comparative Balance Sheet		
37	As of December 31, 2004 and 2003		
38	Assets	2004	2003
39	Cash	$34,830	$63,000
40	Accounts receivable	232,500	298,575
41	Merchandise inventory	825,480	637,500
42	Prepaid expenses	22,500	25,500
43	Plant assets (net)	1,800,000	1,530,000
44	Total assets	$2,915,310	$2,554,575
45			
46	Liabilities & Stockholders' Equity		
47	Accounts payable	$326,400	$339,180
48	Bonds payable, 10% due 2010	360,000	195,000
49	Total liabilities	$686,400	$534,180
50	Common stock	$600,300	$600,300
51	Retained earnings	1,628,610	1,420,095
52	Total stockholders' equity	$2,228,910	$2,020,395
53	Total liabilities & stockholders' equity	$2,915,310	$2,554,575
54			

	A	B	C
55	Answer Section		
56			
57	Liquidity ratios:		
58	Acid-test (quick) ratio		FORMULA1
59	Current ratio		FORMULA2
60	Activity ratios:		
61	Accounts receivable turnover		FORMULA3
62	Inventory turnover		FORMULA4
63	Profitability ratios:		
64	Gross profit ratio		FORMULA5
65	Net income to sales		FORMULA6
66	Rate earned on total assets		FORMULA7
67	Rate earned on common stock equity		FORMULA8
68	Coverage ratios:		
69	Debt to total assets		FORMULA9
70	Times interest earned		FORMULA10
71			

P16 ♦ MANUFACTURING ACCOUNTING (MFG)

LEARNING OBJECTIVES

- Prepare a schedule of cost of goods manufactured and sold.
- Calculate changes in labor cost needed to achieve production goals.
- Alter the worksheet to include an income statement for a manufacturing firm.
- Create a chart showing the dollar amount of materials, labor, and overhead.

PROBLEM DATA

The following information is for Virtual Manufacturing for the year ended December 31, 2004:

Depreciation—equipment	$ 45,000
Direct labor	642,000
Direct materials inventory, 1/1/04	91,500
Direct materials inventory, 12/31/04	93,000
Factory rent	76,410
Finished goods, 1/1/04	132,000
Finished goods, 12/31/04	172,500
Indirect labor	37,500
Indirect materials	26,250
Purchases of direct materials	645,180
Work in process, 1/1/04	30,300
Work in process, 12/31/04	28,665

REQUIRED

1. You have been asked to prepare a schedule of cost of goods manufactured and sold for the year just ended. Review the worksheet MFG that follows these requirements.

2. Using the spaces provided, write the formulas and titles where requested.

FORMULA1_____   FORMULA6_____

FORMULA2_____   FORMULA7_____

FORMULA3_____   FORMULA8_____

FORMULA4_____   FORMULA9_____

FORMULA5_____   FORMULA10_____

FORMULA11_____   FORMULA12_____

TITLE A_____   TITLE E_____

TITLE B_____   TITLE F_____

TITLE C_____   TITLE G_____

TITLE D_____   TITLE H_____

3. Start the spreadsheet program and open the file MFG from the Student Disk. Enter the formulas and titles where requested on the worksheet. The cells that contain zeros now will change to non-zero values as formulas are entered. Enter your name in cell A1. Save the file as MFG3. Print the worksheet when done. Also print your formulas. *Check figure: Cost of goods sold (cell D46), $1,431,975.*

WHAT-IF ANALYSIS

4. The following data pertains to 2005 activities of Virtual Manufacturing:

Depreciation—equipment	$ 46,500
Direct labor	664,500
Direct materials inventory, 12/31/05	85,050
Factory rent	81,000
Finished goods, 12/31/05	181,500
Indirect labor	42,000
Indirect materials	30,000
Purchases of direct materials	603,300
Work in process, 12/31/05	27,225

Use your completed worksheet to determine the firm's cost of goods sold for 2005. Remember to change the year in row 24. Save the 2005 file as MFG4. Print the worksheet when done.

If sales and other expenses were identical in 2004 and 2005, during which year did Virtual earn more income? Why?

CHART ANALYSIS

5. Open MFG3 and click the Chart sheet tab. The management of Virtual is convinced that the quality of their products is highly dependent on their relative labor costs. Experience has shown that direct labor should account for at least 45% of the total product cost. From the pie chart that appears on the screen, Virtual did not achieve this goal in 2004. How much should Virtual have spent on direct labor to reach its 45% goal?

To find out, try different values for direct labor (cell C8), clicking the Chart sheet tab after each attempt. When you find a direct labor level that increases the direct labor percentage to 45%, enter the answer below:

In 2004, direct labor needed to be $_____.

Open MFG4 and click the Chart sheet tab. Did Virtual achieve its 45% goal in 2005? If not, answer the following:

In 2005, direct labor needed to be $_____.

When the assignment is complete, close the files without saving them again.

TICKLERS (optional)

Worksheet. The MFG3 worksheet presents the company's manufacturing activities for 2004. The company also had the following selling and general activities in 2004: sales of $3,375,750, selling expenses of $600,000, and general expenses of $300,000. Modify the worksheet to include this information in the Data Section and change the Answer Section so that it is in the form of an income statement. Use the Print Preview command (File menu) to make sure that the worksheet will print neatly on one page, then print the worksheet. Save the completed file as MFGT.

Hint: Expand the Data Section to include these additional input items alphabetically. Insert a row for sales under the heading in the Answer Section. Add the rest of the income statement information to the bottom of the schedule. You will need to enter formulas for gross profit, all the expenses, and net income. You will also need to change the statement name.

Chart. Using the MFG3 file, prepare a 3-D bar chart to show the dollar amount of materials, labor, and overhead incurred by Virtual in 2004 and 2005. Complete the Chart Data Table and use it as a basis for preparing the chart. Enter all appropriate titles, legends, and formats. Put your name somewhere on the chart. Save the file again as MFG3. Print the chart.

	A	B	C	D
2		MFG		
3		Manufacturing Accounting		
4				
5		Data Section		
6				
7	Depreciation--equipment		$45,000	
8	Direct labor		642,000	
9	Direct materials inventory, 1/1		91,500	
10	Direct materials inventory, 12/31		93,000	
11	Factory rent		76,410	
12	Finished goods, 1/1		132,000	
13	Finished goods, 12/31		172,500	
14	Indirect labor		37,500	
15	Indirect materials		26,250	
16	Purchases of direct materials		645,180	
17	Work in process, 1/1		30,300	
18	Work in process, 12/31		28,665	
19				
20		Answer Section		
21				
22		Virtual Manufacturing		
23		Schedule of Cost of Goods Manufactured and Sold		
24		For the Year Ended December 31, 2000		
25				
26	Direct materials			
27	Direct materials inventory, 1/1			$91,500
28	Add: TITLE A			FORMULA1
29	Cost of direct materials available			$0
30	Less: TITLE B			FORMULA2
31	Cost of direct materials used			FORMULA3
32	Direct labor			642,000
33	Manufacturing overhead:			
34	Factory rent		$76,410	
35	TITLE C		FORMULA4	
36	TITLE D		FORMULA5	
37	TITLE E		FORMULA6	0
38	Total manufacturing costs			FORMULA7
39	Work in process, 1/1			30,300
40	Total work in process available			$0
41	Less: TITLE F			FORMULA8
42	Cost of goods manufactured			FORMULA9
43	TITLE G			FORMULA10
44	Cost of goods available for sale			FORMULA11
45	Less: Finished goods, 12/31			172,500
46	TITLE H			FORMULA12
47				

P17 ♦ JOB ORDER COSTING (JOB)

LEARNING OBJECTIVES
- Develop a job order cost sheet for a manufacturer.
- Record the costs for four jobs.
- Prepare journal entries to record the activity. Post to T-accounts. Reconcile the results to the job order sheets.
- Analyze cost control on the jobs.
- Alter the job order cost sheet to include additional direct materials.
- Create a bar chart showing the cost components of a job.

PROBLEM DATA

AKP Manufacturing Company produces special computer covers made to customer specifications. During August, AKP incurred the following manufacturing costs: direct materials, $28,019.00; direct labor, $15,276.75; and applied factory overhead, $9,854.50. The following data pertain to these costs:

SUMMARY OF DIRECT MATERIAL REQUISITIONS

Dept. No.	Job No.	Req. No.	Quantity	Cost per Unit
1	9011	B766	2,675	$ 2.23
2	9012	B767	125	18.78
1	9013	B768	780	8.29
1	9011	B769	280	5.72
2	9013	B770	95	22.07
1	9014	B771	2,945	3.24

SUMMARY OF DIRECT LABOR TIME TICKETS

Dept. No.	Job No.	Ticket Nos.	Hours	Rate per Hour
1	9011	1056-1166	770	$7.25
1	9012	1167-1173	50	7.25
2	9012	2121-2130	92	8.75
1	9013	1174-1189	178	7.25
2	9013	2131-2134	44	8.75
1	9014	1190-1230	945	7.25

The overhead application rates are $4 per direct labor hour for Dept. 1 and 175% of direct labor cost for Dept. 2.

AKP had no beginning work in process for August. Job 9008, which cost $14,190.18 to manufacture, was completed in July and was sold on account in August for $19,000. The job cost sheet for this job is shown on page 123.

Of the jobs begun in August, Job 9011 was completed and sold on account for $24,000, Job 9012 and 9014 were completed but not sold, and Job 9013 was still in process.

REQUIRED

1. As cost accountant for this company, you have been asked to prepare job cost sheets for each of the four jobs started in August. Review the printed worksheet called JOB that follows these requirements. There are 13 fairly simple formulas to enter on this worksheet.

2. Using the printout of Job 9008 as an example, write the appropriate formulas in the spaces provided below. FORMULA1 has been written for you.

FORMULA1_____=E12*F12_____   FORMULA8_____

FORMULA2_____   FORMULA9_____

FORMULA3_____   FORMULA10_____

FORMULA4_____   FORMULA11_____

FORMULA5_____   FORMULA12_____

FORMULA6_____   FORMULA13_____

FORMULA7_____

3. Start the spreadsheet program and open the file JOB from the Student Disk. Enter the 13 formulas in the appropriate cells on the worksheet. This worksheet will be used to compute the total cost of each job worked on. It will simplify matters to save the completed version of JOB before entering specific job data on it. Save your empty worksheet with the formulas on it as JOBX. Also print your formulas.

WHAT-IF ANALYSIS

4. Now that your worksheet has been saved as JOBX, fill in the appropriate data for Job 9011. Save the results as JOB9011 and print the completed job cost sheet when done. *Check figure: Cost of Job 9011 (cell G31), $16,229.35.*

5. Next, open worksheet JOBX again. Enter the data for Job 9012, save the results as JOB9012, and print the worksheet. Repeat these steps for Jobs 9013 and 9014.

6. Use the space provided below to prepare summary journal entries for the month of August. Then set up T-accounts for Work in Process, Finished Goods, Cost of Goods Sold, and Sales. Post the entries to the appropriate accounts and then balance each account. Finally, prepare a supporting schedule by job number showing the cost of ending work in process, finished goods, and cost of goods sold.

CHART ANALYSIS

7. AKP's management is very concerned about the cost of labor on its jobs. When jobs are complete, labor costs should be between 30 and 35% of total costs. For example, the labor cost on Job 9008 is 37% of total costs. Open Job 9011 and click the Chart sheet tab. A pie chart appears showing the cost components on that job. Record the labor cost percentage below. Repeat this for each of the jobs worked on in August.

Job #	Labor %
9011	_____
9012	_____
9013	_____
9014	_____

Did AKP maintain good cost control on all its jobs? Explain.

TICKLERS (optional)

Worksheet. During September, Job 9013 required two additional material requisitions to complete the job. Open JOB9013 and modify the job cost sheet to include an area for four direct material requisition entries instead of three. Then enter the following two materials requisitions onto the worksheet:

Dept. #	Job #	Req. #	Quantity	Cost/Unit
1	9013	B772	1,200	$ .45
2	9013	B774	55	22.50

Save the completed worksheet as JOBT. Print the results.

Chart. Open JOB9011 and click the Chart sheet tab. Prepare a bar chart for JOB9011 showing the amount of material, labor, and overhead required to complete the job. Use the Chart Data Table found in rows 42–46 as a basis for preparing the chart. Put your name somewhere on the chart. Save the file again as JOB9011. Print the chart.

	A	B	C	D	E	F	G
1							
2				*JOB*			
3				*Job Order Costing*			
4							
5						Job No.	9008
6							
7				*AKP Manufacturing Company*			
8				*Job Cost Sheet*			
9							
10				*Direct Materials*			
11		Dept. #	Req. #		Quantity	Cost/Unit	Total
12		1	B755		965	2.02	*$1,949.30*
13		1	B757		785	1.05	*824.25*
14		2	B763		30	85.20	*2,556.00*
15						Total	*$5,329.55*
16							
17				*Direct Labor*			
18		Dept. #	Ticket #		Hours	Rate	Total
19		1	948-992		655	7.25	*$4,748.75*
20		2	2112-2119		62	8.75	*542.50*
21						Total	*$5,291.25*
22							
23				*Applied Factory Overhead*			
24		Dept. #	Basis	Hours	Cost	Rate	Total
25		1	DL hours	*655*	XXXX	$4	*$2,620.00*
26		2	DL cost	XXXXX	*542.50*	175%	*949.38*
27						Total	*$3,569.38*
28							
29				*Total Factory Cost*			
30							
31						Total	*$14,190.18*
32							

	A	B	C	D	E	F	G
2				*JOB*			
3				*Job Order Costing*			
4							
5						Job No.	XXXX
6							
7				*AKP Manufacturing Company*			
8				*Job Cost Sheet*			
9							
10				*Direct Materials*			
11		Dept. #	Req. #		Quantity	Cost/Unit	Total
12							*FORMULA1*
13							*FORMULA2*
14							*FORMULA3*
15						Total	*FORMULA4*
16							
17				*Direct Labor*			
18		Dept. #	Ticket #		Hours	Rate	Total
19		1					*FORMULA5*
20		2					*FORMULA6*
21						Total	*FORMULA7*
22							
23				*Applied Factory Overhead*			
24		Dept. #	Basis	Hours	Cost	Rate	Total
25		1	DL hours	*FORMULA8*	XXXX	$ 4	*FORMULA10*
26		2	DL cost	XXXXX	*FORMULA9*	175%	*FORMULA11*
27						Total	*FORMULA12*
28							
29				*Total Factory Cost*			
30							
31						Total	*FORMULA13*
32							

P18 ♦ COST-VOLUME-PROFIT ANALYSIS (CVP)

LEARNING OBJECTIVES

- Develop a cost-volume-profit analysis model.
- Calculate contribution margin, contribution margin ratio, break-even point, and projected income.
- Determine the effect of changes in price, variable costs, and fixed costs.
- Interpret the information provided by cost-volume-profit charts.
- Alter the worksheet to include an income statement in contribution margin format.
- Create a profit/volume chart.

PROBLEM DATA

Condor Manufacturing, which maintains the same level of inventory at the end of each year, provided the following information about expenses anticipated for 2005:

	Fixed Expenses	Variable Expenses (per unit sold)
Production costs:		
Direct materials		$ 4.30
Direct labor		4.70
Factory overhead	$225,000	3.00
Selling expenses:		
Sales salaries and commissions	97,000	.75
Advertising	47,500	
Miscellaneous selling expense	16,200	
General expenses:		
Office salaries	87,000	
Supplies	12,300	1.25
Miscellaneous general expense	15,000	
	$500,000	$14.00

The selling price of Condor's single product is $20. In recent years, profits have fallen and Condor's management is now considering a number of alternatives. For 2005, Condor wants to have a net income of $200,000, but expects to sell only 90,000 units unless some changes are made.

REQUIRED

1. The president of Condor has asked you to calculate the company's projected net income (assuming 90,000 units are sold) and the sales needed to achieve the company's net income objective for 2005. Also, compute Condor's contribution margin per unit, contribution margin ratio, and break-even point for 2005. The worksheet CVP has been provided to assist you. Note that the data from the problem have already been entered into the Data Section of the worksheet.

2. In the spaces provided below, write the seven formulas requested in the worksheet.

   FORMULA1_____   FORMULA5_____

   FORMULA2_____   FORMULA6_____

   FORMULA3_____   FORMULA7_____

   FORMULA4_____

3. Start the spreadsheet program and open the file CVP from the Student Disk. Enter the formulas where indicated on the worksheet. Enter your name in cell A1. Save the solution as CVP3 and print the worksheet. Also print your formulas. *Check figure: Break-even point in sales dollars (cell C34), $1,666,667.*

4. Based on Condor's current situation, will it earn its target net income? If not, how many units need to be sold to achieve the target? Explain.

WHAT-IF ANALYSIS

5. The president of Condor would like to know the effect that each of the following suggestions for improving performance would have on contribution margin per unit, sales needed to break even, and projected net income for 2005. Each change should be considered independently. Reset the Data Section to its original values after each suggestion is analyzed. Fill in the table following the suggestions with the results of your analysis.

   a. The president suggests cutting the product's price. Since the market is relatively sensitive to price, ". . . a 10% cut in price ought to generate a 30% increase in sales. How can you lose?"

   b. The sales manager feels that putting all sales personnel on straight commission would help. This would eliminate $77,000 in fixed sales salaries expense; variable sales commissions would increase to $2.00 per unit. This move would also increase sales volume by 30%.

c. Condor's head of product engineering wants to redesign the package for the product. This will cut $1.00 per unit from direct materials and $0.50 per unit from direct labor, but will increase fixed factory overhead by $10,000 for additional depreciation on the new packaging machine. The package redesign would not affect sales volume.

d. The firm's consumer marketing manager suggests undertaking a new advertising campaign on cable TV. This would cost $30,000 more than is currently planned for advertising but would be expected to increase sales volume by 30%.

e. The production superintendent suggests raising quality and raising price. This will increase direct materials by $1.00 per unit, direct labor by $0.50 per unit, and fixed factory overhead by $40,000. With improved quality, ". . . raise the price to $22 and advertise the heck out of it. If you double your current planned advertising, I'll bet you can increase your sales volume by 30%."

	Contribution Margin per Unit	Break-even Point (units)	Projected Net Income
original data			
a.			
b.			
c.			
d.			
e.			

6. From this analysis, should Condor use any of the suggestions?

7. The president of Condor can't figure out where his math went wrong. Explain it to him. Also compute how many units would have to be sold at $18 in order for the firm to achieve its target net income of $200,000.

CHART ANALYSIS

8. Reset the Data Section to its initial values and click the Chart sheet tab. On the screen you will see a cost-volume-profit chart (also commonly called a break-even chart). In the space provided below, identify the names of the data ranges.

       Data range A _____

       Data range B _____

       Data range C _____

Use the chart to answer the following questions:

a. What is the approximate break-even point in units?

b. What is the approximate profit or loss if Condor sells 40,000 units?

c. What dollar amount of fixed factory overhead would push the break-even point to 100,000 units? (*Hint:* enter different amounts in cell B11 and click the Chart sheet tab until the desired result is achieved.)

d. What selling price would push the break-even point to 100,000 units?

When the assignment is complete, close the file without saving it again.

TICKLERS (optional)

Worksheet. Condor's controller would like to have the worksheet display an income statement in a contribution margin format (Sales – variable costs = contribution margin – fixed costs = net income). Using the CVP3 file, begin the statement in column E. Use the Print Preview command (File menu) to make sure that the statement will print neatly on one page, then print the statement. Save the completed file as CVPT.

Chart. Using the CVP3 file, create a line chart in which profit or loss is plotted on the Y-axis and sales volume is plotted on the X-axis. This is commonly called a profit/volume chart. Although sales volume can be expressed in either units or dollars, use units for your chart. Revise the Chart Data Table to include a column for profits. Use this table as a basis for preparing the chart. Put your name somewhere on the chart. Save the file again as CVP3. Print the chart.

	A	B	C
2	CVP		
3	Cost-Volume-Profit Analysis		
4			
5	Data Section		
6			
7		Fixed	Variable
8	Production costs		
9	Direct materials		$4.30
10	Direct labor		4.70
11	Factory overhead	$225,000	3.00
12	Selling expenses		
13	Sales salaries & commissions	97,000	0.75
14	Advertising	47,500	
15	Miscellaneous selling expense	16,200	
16	General expenses		
17	Office salaries	87,000	
18	Supplies	12,300	1.25
19	Miscellaneous general expense	15,000	
20		$500,000	$14.00
21			
22	Projected unit sales		90,000
23	Selling price per unit		$20.00
24	Target net income		$200,000
25			
26	Answer Section		
27			
28	Contribution margin per unit		FORMULA1
29	Contribution margin ratio		FORMULA2
30			
31	Break-even point in units		FORMULA3
32	Units needed to achieve target net income		FORMULA4
33			
34	Break-even point in dollars		FORMULA5
35	Sales dollars needed to achieve target net income		FORMULA6
36			
37	Net income based on projected unit sales (cell C22)		FORMULA7
38			

P19 ♦ VARIABLE COSTING (VARCOST)

LEARNING OBJECTIVES

- Prepare variable costing and absorption costing income statements.
- Reconcile the differences between absorption and variable costing net income.
- Contrast the effects of production levels on absorption and variable costing net income.
- Alter the worksheet to allow it to handle sales in excess of production.
- Create a chart plotting absorption costing income and variable costing income.

PROBLEM DATA

The records of Mae Manufacturing contain the following information for the month of August:

Actual production in units	100,000
Sales in units	80,000
Sales price per unit	$30
Variable manufacturing cost per unit	14
Variable selling expense per unit	2
Fixed manufacturing cost	630,000
Fixed selling expenses	100,000

The company has no beginning inventory.

REQUIRED

1. You have been asked to prepare a variable costing (direct costing) income statement and an absorption costing income statement for the month of August. Review the worksheet VARCOST that follows these requirements.

2. Using the spaces provided below, write the 10 formulas requested. FORMULA1 has been written for you as an example.

FORMULA1_____=B8*B9_____   FORMULA6_____

FORMULA2_____   FORMULA7_____

FORMULA3_____   FORMULA8_____

FORMULA4_____   FORMULA9_____

FORMULA5_____   FORMULA10_____

3. Start the spreadsheet program and open the file VARCOST from the Student Disk. Enter the formulas where indicated on the worksheet. Enter your name in cell A1. Save the completed file as VARCOST3. Print the worksheet when done. Also print your formulas. *Check figure: Absorption income (cell C31), $516,000.*

4. In the space below, explain why the operating income calculated by the absorption method is not the same as that calculated by the variable cost method.

WHAT-IF ANALYSIS

5. To determine the effect of different levels of production on the company's income, move to cell B7 (Actual Production). Change the number in B7 to the different production levels given in the table below. The first level, 100,000, is the current level. What happens to operating income on both statements as production levels change? Enter the operating incomes in the table below.

August Operating Income	Production Level 100,000	90,000	80,000
Absorption	$_____	$_____	$_____
Variable	$_____	$_____	$_____

Does the level of production affect income under either costing method? Explain your findings.

CHART ANALYSIS

6. Click the Chart sheet tab. This chart is based on the problem data and the two income statements. Answer the following questions about the chart:

   a. What is the title for the X-axis?

   b. What is the title for the Y-axis?

   c. What does data range A represent?

d.   What does data range B represent?

e.   Why do the two data ranges cross?

f.   What would be a good title for this chart?

When the assignment is complete, close the file without saving it again.

TICKLERS (optional)

Worksheet. The VARCOST3 worksheet is capable of calculating variable and absorption income when unit sales are equal to or less than production. An equally common situation (that this worksheet cannot handle) is when beginning inventory is present and sales volume exceeds production volume. Revise the worksheet Data Section to include:

Beginning inventory in units	15,000
Beginning inventory cost (absorption)	$304,500
Beginning inventory cost (variable)	$210,000

Also, change actual production to 70,000.

Revise the Answer Section to accommodate this new data. Assume that Mae Manufacturing uses the weighted average costing method for inventory. Use the Print Preview command (File menu) to make sure that the worksheet will print neatly on one page, then print the worksheet. Save the completed file as VARCOSTT. *Check figure: Absorption income, $338,118.*

Chart. Using the VARCOST3 file, fix up the chart used in requirement 6 by adding appropriate titles and legends and formatting the X- and Y-axes. Put your name somewhere on the chart. Save the file again as VARCOST3. Print the chart.

	A	B	C
1			
2	**VARCOST**		
3	Variable Costing		
4			
5	Data Section		
6			
7	Actual production in units	100,000	
8	Sales in units	80,000	
9	Sales price per unit	$30	
10	Variable manufacturing costs per unit	$14	
11	Variable selling costs per unit	$2	
12	Fixed manufacturing costs	$630,000	
13	Fixed selling expenses	$100,000	
14			
15	Answer Section		
16			
17	Income statement: Absorption costing		
18			
19	Sales		FORMULA1
20	Cost of goods sold:		
21	Variable manufacturing costs	FORMULA2	
22	Fixed manufacturing costs	FORMULA3	
23	Total goods available for sale	$0	
24	Less ending inventory	FORMULA4	
25	Cost of goods sold		0
26	Gross profit		$0
27	Selling expenses:		
28	Fixed selling expenses	FORMULA5	
29	Variable selling expenses	FORMULA6	
30	Total selling expenses		0
31	Operating income		$0
32			
33			
34	Income statement: Variable costing		
35			
36	Sales		$0
37	Cost of goods sold:		
38	Variable manufacturing costs	FORMULA7	
39	Less ending inventory	FORMULA8	
40	Variable cost of goods sold		0
41	Manufacturing margin		$0
42	Variable selling expenses		FORMULA9
43	Contribution margin		$0
44	Fixed costs:		
45	Fixed manufacturing costs	FORMULA10	
46	Fixed selling expenses	0	
47	Total fixed costs		0
48	Operating income		$0
49			

P20 ◆ ACTIVITY-BASED COSTING (ABC)

LEARNING OBJECTIVES

- Calculate pool rates and product costs using ABC.
- Interpret changes in cost resulting from changes in activity.
- Identify components of product cost.
- Alter the worksheet to include one new product.
- Modify a stacked-column chart by adding titles, legends, and formats.

PROBLEM DATA

Denton Micronics Company manufactures Scanners and Radar Detectors. They have identified the following overhead costs and related cost drivers for the coming year.

Overhead Item	Expected Cost	Cost Driver	Amount
Setup costs	$240,000	Number of setups	600
Ordering costs	90,000	Number of orders	9,000
Machine costs	180,000	Machine hours	36,000
Power	50,000	Kilowatt hours	100,000

The following were incurred in manufacturing Scanners and Radar Detectors during the first quarter.

	Scanner	Radar Detector
Direct materials	$1,300	$1,525
Direct labor	$900	$900
Units completed	80	50
Number of setups	2	1
Number of orders	6	3
Machine hours	30	40
Kilowatt hours	40	50

REQUIRED

1. Review the worksheet called ABC that follows these requirements. Determine the cost of each product using an activity-based cost system. Note that the problem information is already entered into the Data Section of the ABC worksheet.

2. Using the spaces provided below, enter the 14 formulas required to complete the worksheet. FORMULA1 has been written for you as an example.

FORMULA1 _____ **=B8/E8** _____   FORMULA8 _____

FORMULA2 _____   FORMULA9 _____

FORMULA3 _____   FORMULA10 _____

FORMULA4 _____   FORMULA11 _____

FORMULA5 _____   FORMULA12 _____

FORMULA6 _____   FORMULA13 _____

FORMULA7 _____   FORMULA14 _____

3. Start the spreadsheet program and open the file ABC from the Student Disk. Enter the formulas in the appropriate cells on the worksheet. Enter your name in cell A1. Save your completed file as ABC3. Print the worksheet. Also print your formulas. *Check figure: Cost per unit of Scanners (cell B43), $40.38.*

WHAT-IF ANALYSIS

4. Denton Micronics Company is trying to reduce its unit costs. Management believes that the two areas to save costs are setups and power. Determine the new cost information for each of the following independent situations. Remember to reset your data to the original information after answering each item.

   a. What are the new unit costs of each product if annual setup costs are reduced by 25%?

   Scanners: _____   Radar Detectors: _____

   b. What is the new unit cost of Scanners if the number of setups can be reduced by 50% (to one)?

   Scanners: _____

   c. What is the new unit cost of each product if annual power costs are reduced by 70%?

   Scanners: _____   Radar Detectors: _____

5. Which one of the above would create the lowest cost of Scanners? Why?

CHART ANALYSIS

6. Open ABC3 and click the Chart sheet tab. The stacked-column chart on the screen is based on the program data and your answers.

    a. Identify what this chart describes.

    b. What does each section of the bars represent?

        A_____

        B_____

        C_____

        D_____

    c. What would be an appropriate title for this chart?

TICKLERS (optional)

Worksheet. Extend the Data Section and the Answer Section of ABC3 to include a third product, Digital Pagers, using the information below. Use the Print Preview command to make sure that the worksheet will print neatly on one page, then print the worksheet. Save the completed worksheet as ABCT.

	Digital Pagers
Direct materials	$1,250
Direct labor	$800
Units completed	60
Number of setups	3
Number of orders	2
Machine hours	35
Kilowatt hours	60

Chart. Using the ABC3 file, fix up the chart used in requirement 6 by adding appropriate titles and legends, and an appropriate format for the Y-axis. Put your name somewhere on the chart. Save the file again as ABC3. Print the chart.

	A	B	C	D	E
2			*ABC*		
3			*Activity-Based Costing*		
4					
5	Data Section				
6					
7	Overhead Item	Expected Cost		Cost Driver	Amount
8	Setup costs	$240,000		Number of setups	600
9	Ordering costs	90,000		Number of orders	9,000
10	Machine costs	180,000		Machine hours	36,000
11	Power	50,000		Kilowatt hours	100,000
12					
13			Radar		
14		Scanners	Detectors		
15	Direct materials	$1,300	$1,525		
16	Direct labor	$900	$900		
17	Units completed	80	50		
18	Number of setups	2	1		
19	Number of orders	6	3		
20	Machine hours	30	40		
21	Kilowatt hours	40	50		
22					
23	Answer Section				
24					
25		Pool Rates			
26	Setup	FORMULA1	per setup		
27	Ordering	FORMULA2	per order		
28	Machine Costs	FORMULA3	per machine hour		
29	Power	FORMULA4	per kilowatt hour		
30					
31		Product Costs			
32			Radar		
33		Scanners	Detectors		
34	Direct materials	$1,300	$1,525		
35	Direct labor	900	900		
36	Overhead				
37	Setups	FORMULA5	FORMULA6		
38	Ordering	FORMULA7	FORMULA8		
39	Machine costs	FORMULA9	FORMULA10		
40	Power	FORMULA11	FORMULA12		
41	Total cost	$2,200	$2,425		
42					
43	Unit cost	FORMULA13	FORMULA14		
44					

P21 ♦ CASH BUDGETING (CASHBUD)

LEARNING OBJECTIVES

- Prepare a cash budget for a merchandising firm.
- Analyze several options to improve cash flow.
- Compare cash flow and net income trends.
- Modify the worksheet to include an additional time period.
- Create a line chart comparing cash receipts and disbursements.

PROBLEM DATA

On January 1, Mandy Mat, Inc. begins business. The company has $6,000 cash on hand and is attempting to project cash receipts and disbursements through April 30. On May 1, a note payable of $4,000 will be due. This amount was borrowed on January 1 to carry the company through its first four months of operations.

The unit purchase cost of the company's single product, a Mandy Mat, is $6. The unit sales price is $14.50. Projected purchases and sales in units for the first four months are:

	Purchases	Sales
January	1,200	600
February	1,300	1,200
March	1,400	1,400
April	1,700	1,500

Sales terms call for a 2% discount if paid within the same month that the sale occurred. It is expected that 50% of the billings will be collected within the discount period, 25% by the end of the month after purchase, 20% in the following month, and 5% will be uncollectible.

All purchases are payable within 15 days. Thus, approximately 50% of the purchases in a month are due and payable in the next month.

Total fixed marketing and administrative expenses for each month include cash expenses of $2,500 and depreciation on equipment of $1,000. Variable marketing and administrative expenses total $3 per unit sold. All marketing and administrative expenses are paid as incurred.

REQUIRED

1. You have been asked to prepare a cash budget for the next four months to see if the loan can be repaid. Review the worksheet CASHBUD that follows these requirements. The problem data have already been entered in the Data Section of the worksheet.

2. To complete the cash budget for the four-month period, there are eight formulas to be entered. Using the spaces provided below, write the formulas requested. The cells containing zeros are preprogrammed and will be automatically calculated as the worksheet is completed.

   FORMULA1 _____   FORMULA5 _____

   FORMULA2 _____   FORMULA6 _____

   FORMULA3 _____   FORMULA7 _____

   FORMULA4 _____   FORMULA8 _____

3. Start the spreadsheet program and open the file CASHBUD from the Student Disk. Enter the eight formulas where indicated on the worksheet. Enter your name in cell A1. Save the file as CASHBUD3. Print the worksheet when done. Also print your formulas. *Check figure: Ending cash balance for April (cell E54), $3,614.*

4. Can the $4,000 note be repaid on May 1? Explain.

5. How do the other months look? Are any problems coming? Explain.

WHAT-IF ANALYSIS

6. The following four suggestions have been made to improve the company's cash position. Evaluate the effect on cash flow for each of the four suggestions. After evaluating each suggestion, enter the projected cash balances in the spaces provided. Consider each suggestion separately. Reset cells to their initial values after each new suggestion.

   a. Seek agreement with suppliers to extend the credit period from 15 to 30 days. This would mean that all current monthly purchases would be paid for in the following month.

   b. Raise the unit price from $14.50 to $15.50. A price increase will reduce unit sales by 10% each month. Purchases will also be reduced by 10%.

   c. Put the company's two salespeople on straight commission. This would reduce fixed marketing and administrative costs to $750 per month and raise variable marketing and administrative costs to $4 per unit.

   d. Increase the cash discount from 2% to 4%. It is anticipated that this would increase the percentage of customers paying within the discount period to 85%, and those paying the month after the discount period would drop to 8%. Five percent would pay in the following month and 2% would still be uncollectible.

   ### PROJECTED ENDING CASH BALANCES

	January	February	March	April
A	_____	_____	_____	_____
B	_____	_____	_____	_____
C	_____	_____	_____	_____
D	_____	_____	_____	_____

   What are your recommendations for Mandy Mat, Inc.? Consider potential impact on profits as well as cash balances.

7. Reset cells to their initial values. Mandy Mat, Inc. is considering undertaking a $1,200 per month advertising campaign to promote the Mandy Mat as an exclusive, high-fashion item for the home. What price (dollars and cents) would Mandy have to charge for each mat to be able to pay for the campaign, pay back the $4,000 note, and have $5,000 left over at the end of April?

   Sales Price $ _____

CHART ANALYSIS

8. Open CASHBUD3 and click the Chart sheet tab. A chart appears that plots the relationship between monthly unit sales, unit purchases, and ending cash balance. What happens to ending cash balance if January purchases are reduced to 1,100 units? Enter 1,100 in cell C22 on the worksheet and then check the chart. What about 1,000 units? 900 units? 800 units? Enter your observations below. Is this a possible solution to the company's potential cash problem?

TICKLERS (optional)

Worksheet. Extend the CASHBUD3 worksheet to include the month of May. May sales are expected to be 1,500 units and purchases are to be 1,400 units. Also show the repayment of the loan on May 1. Set the print commands to have the worksheet print on a single page. Save the completed worksheet as CASHBUDT. Print the new budget.

Chart. Use CASHBUD3 to create a line chart plotting total monthly receipts and monthly disbursements over the four-month period. Put your name somewhere on the chart. Save the file again as CASHBUD3. Print the chart.

	A	B	C	D	E
2	CASHBUD				
3	Cash Budgeting				
4					
5	Data Section				
6					
7	Beginning cash balance, January 1		$6,000		
8	Sales:				
9	Unit sales price		$14.50		
10	January estimated units		600		
11	February estimated units		1,200		
12	March estimated units		1,400		
13	April estimated units		1,500		
14	Collections:				
15	Cash discount (%)		2%		
16	% Collected current month		50%		
17	% Collected next month		25%		
18	% Collected following month		20%		
19	% Uncollectible		5%		
20	Purchases:				
21	Unit purchase cost		$6		
22	January planned purchases (units)		1,200		
23	February planned purchases (units)		1,300		
24	March planned purchases (units)		1,400		
25	April planned purchases (units)		1,700		
26	% Paid in month purchased		50%		
27	% Paid in month after purchase		50%		
28	Marketing & administrative:				
29	Fixed cash expenses per month		$2,500		
30	Depreciation per month		$1,000		
31	Variable cost per unit sold		$3		
32					

	A	B	C	D	E
33	Answer Section				
34					
35		Mandy Mat Inc.			
36		Cash Budget			
37					
38		January	February	March	April
39	Cash balance, beginning	FORMULA1	$0	$0	$0
40	Add receipts:				
41	Collections January sales	FORMULA2	FORMULA3	FORMULA4	
42	Collections February sales		0	0	0
43	Collections March sales			0	0
44	Collections April sales				0
45	Total available	$0	$0	$0	$0
46	Less disbursements:				
47	Purchases made in January	FORMULA5	FORMULA6		
48	Purchases made in February		0	$0	
49	Purchases made in March			0	$0
50	Purchases made in April				0
51	Fixed marketing & admin.	FORMULA7	0	0	0
52	Variable marketing & admin.	FORMULA8	0	0	0
53	Total disbursements	$0	$0	$0	$0
54	Cash balance, ending	$0	$0	$0	$0
55					

P22 ♦ MASTER BUDGET (MASTER)

LEARNING OBJECTIVES

• Develop a master budget including a balance sheet, income statement, and cash budget.
• Interpret the budgets and the differences between profit and cash flow.
• Contrast the effects of changes in projected sales on the budgets.
• Alter the worksheet by adding a column to show quarterly totals.
• Create a chart showing projected sales.

PROBLEM DATA

Quest Industries has provided the following information at May 31, 2005:

Unit Sales, 2005

April	1,500	actual
May	1,000	actual
June	1,600	budgeted
July	1,400	budgeted
August	1,500	budgeted
September	1,200	budgeted

Balance Sheet, May 31, 2005

Cash	$ 12,300
Accounts receivable	122,500
Merchandise inventory (640 units)	35,200
Fixed assets (net)	130,000
Total assets	$300,000
Accounts payable (merchandise)	$ 74,800
Owner's equity	225,200
Total liabilities and equity	$300,000

Other information:

Average selling price, $98
Average purchase price per unit, $55
Desired ending inventory, 40% of next month's unit sales
Collections from customers:

In month of sale	20%
In month after sale	50%
Two months after sale	30%

Projected cash payments:

    Inventory purchases are paid for in month following acquisition.

    Variable cash expenses, other than inventory, are equal to 25% of each month's sales
       and are paid in month of sale.

    Fixed cash expenses are $20,000 per month and are paid in month incurred.

    Depreciation on equipment is $1,000 per month.

REQUIRED

1.   You have been asked to prepare a master budget for the upcoming quarter (June, July, and August). The components of this budget are a monthly sales budget, a monthly purchases budget, a monthly cash budget, a forecasted income statement for the quarter, and a forecasted August 31 balance sheet. The worksheet MASTER has been provided to assist you.

    Quest Industries desires to maintain a minimum cash balance of $8,000 at the end of each month. If this goal cannot be met, the company borrows the exact amount needed to reach its goal. If the company has a cash balance greater than $8,000 and also has loans payable outstanding, the amount in excess of $8,000 is paid to the bank. Annual interest of 18% is paid on a monthly basis on the outstanding balance.

2.   In the spaces provided below, write the formulas requested on the worksheet. FORMULA1 has been provided for you as an example.

FORMULA1 _____**=B10**_____	FORMULA12_____
FORMULA2_____	FORMULA13_____
FORMULA3_____	FORMULA14_____
FORMULA4_____	FORMULA15_____
FORMULA5_____	FORMULA16_____
FORMULA6_____	FORMULA17_____
FORMULA7_____	FORMULA18_____
FORMULA8_____	FORMULA19_____
FORMULA9_____	FORMULA20_____
FORMULA10_____	FORMULA21_____
FORMULA11_____	FORMULA22_____

FORMULA23_____   FORMULA26_____

FORMULA24_____   FORMULA27_____

FORMULA25_____   FORMULA28_____

3.   Start the spreadsheet program and open the file MASTER from the Student Disk. Enter all
     the formulas where indicated on the worksheet. Check to be sure that your balance sheet
     balances. Enter your name in cell A1. Save the completed file as MASTER3. Print the work-
     sheet when done. Also print your formulas using fit-to-1 page scaling. *Check figures: Ex-
     cess (deficit) of cash over needs (cell B76), ($5,240); forecasted net income (cell D95),
     $20,052; total assets (cell D105), $321,152.*

4.   Review the completed master budget and answer the following questions:

     a.   Is Quest Industries expecting to earn a profit during the next quarter? If so, how much?

     b.   Does the company need to borrow cash during the quarter? Can it make any repay-
          ments? Explain. (Carefully review rows 74 through 80.)

     c.   Calculate the debt ratio (total liabilities divided by total assets) for Quest.

WHAT-IF ANALYSIS

5.   Suppose the company has to revise its estimates because of a downturn in the economy.
     Unit sales for July, August, and September will be half (50%) of the original estimates. Re-
     vise the estimates in cells B11 through B13. After this is done, check your forecasted bal-
     ance sheet. It should still balance! What effect will this new state of affairs have on net
     income, borrowing, and debt ratio? Explain why these items changed.

6.   Suppose the company has just the opposite news and now expects unit sales for July, Au-
     gust, and September to be double (200%) the original estimates. What effect will this have
     on the company's net income, borrowing, and debt ratio? Explain your findings.

CHART ANALYSIS

7. Click the Chart sheet tab. You will see a chart plotting sales and net income over a range of sales volumes in July, August, and September (100% equals the original problem data). This is a graphical representation of the sales and net income components of requirements 5 and 6. A review of this chart raises two additional questions about the relationship between sales and net income:

    a. From the chart, estimate sales volumes (roughly), in percentage and dollars, that are required for Quest to break even (net income equals $0) during this quarter.

        Expected volume percent % _____
        Sales (dollars) $_____

    b. Notice that net income is rising slower than sales volume. Is this a problem?

    When the assignment is complete, close the file without saving it again.

TICKLERS (optional)

Worksheet. Quest wants to have each budget on the MASTER3 worksheet not only show monthly figures but also totals for the quarter. Use column E to present totals for all budget lines (except in the budgeted income statement and balance sheet). Consult your textbook for proper treatment of beginning and ending balances in the production, purchases, and cash budgets. Use the Print Preview command (File menu) to make sure that the worksheet including the totals will print out neatly, then print the worksheet. Save the completed file as MASTERT.

Chart. Using the MASTER3 file, create a 3-D area chart to show the monthly sales volume in units, from April through September. No Chart Data Table is needed; use data from the worksheet. Put your name somewhere on the chart. Save the file again as MASTER3. Print the chart.

	A	B	C	D
2	**MASTER**			
3	*Master Budget*			
4				
5	Data Section			
6				
7	Actual and Budgeted Unit Sales			
8	April	1,500		
9	May	1,000		
10	June	1,600		
11	July	1,400		
12	August	1,500		
13	September	1,200		
14				
15	Balance Sheet, May 31, 2005			
16	Cash	$12,300		
17	Accounts receivable	122,500		
18	Merchandise inventory	35,200		
19	Fixed assets (net)	130,000		
20	Total assets	$300,000		
21				
22	Accounts payable (merchandise)	$74,800		
23	Owner's equity	225,200		
24	Total liabilities & equity	$300,000		
25				
26	Other Data			
27	Average selling price	$98		
28	Average purchase cost per unit	$55		
29	Desired ending inventory			
30	(% of next month's unit sales)	40%		
31	Collections from customers:			
32	Collected in month of sale	20%		
33	Collected in month after sale	50%		
34	Collected two months after sale	30%		
35	Projected cash payments:			
36	Variable expenses	25%	of sales	
37	Fixed expenses (per month)	$20,000		
38	Depreciation per month	$1,000		
39				

	A	B	C	D
40	Answer Section			
41				
42	Sales Budget	June	July	August
43	Units	FORMULA1	0	0
44				
45	Dollars	FORMULA2	0	0
46				
47				
48	Unit Purchases Budget	June	July	August
49	Desired ending inventory	FORMULA3	0	0
50	Current month's unit sales	FORMULA4	0	0
51	Total units needed	FORMULA5	0	0
52	Beginning inventory	FORMULA6	0	0
53	Purchases (units)	FORMULA7	0	0
54				
55	Purchases (dollars)	FORMULA8	$0	$0
56				
57				
58	Cash Budget	June	July	August
59	Cash balance, beginning	$12,300	$0	$0
60	Cash receipts:			
61	Collections from customers:			
62	From April sales	FORMULA9		
63	From May sales	FORMULA10	FORMULA11	
64	From June sales	FORMULA12	0	0
65	From July sales		0	0
66	From August sales			0
67	Total cash available	$0	$0	$0
68	Cash disbursements:			
69	Merchandise	FORMULA13	$0	$0
70	Variable expenses	FORMULA14	0	0
71	Fixed expenses	FORMULA15	0	0
72	Interest paid	0	0	0
73	Total disbursements	$0	$0	$0
74	Cash balance before financing	$0	$0	$0
75	Less: Desired ending balance	0	0	0
76	Excess (deficit) of cash over needs	$0	$0	$0
77	Financing			
78	Borrowing	$0	$0	$0
79	Repayment	0	0	0
80	Total effects of financing	$0	$0	$0
81	Cash balance, ending	$0	$0	$0
82				

	A	B	C	D
83				
84	Forecasted Income Statement			
85	For Quarter Ended August 31, 2005			
86	Sales			FORMULA16
87	Cost of goods sold			FORMULA17
88	Gross profit			FORMULA18
89	Expenses:			
90	Variable expenses			FORMULA19
91	Fixed expenses			FORMULA20
92	Depreciation expense			FORMULA21
93	Interest expense			FORMULA22
94	Total expenses			$0
95	Net income			$0
96				
97				
98	Forecasted Balance Sheet			
99	August 31, 2005			
100	Assets:			
101	Cash			FORMULA23
102	Accounts receivable			FORMULA24
103	Merchandise inventory			FORMULA25
104	Fixed assets (net)			FORMULA26
105	Total assets			$0
106				
107	Liabilities & equity:			
108	Accounts payable			FORMULA27
109	Loans payable			0
110	Owner's equity			FORMULA28
111	Total liabilities & equity			$0
112				

P23 ♦ FLEXIBLE BUDGETING (FLEXBUD)

LEARNING OBJECTIVES

*   Prepare a flexible budget for overhead costs.
*   Interpret differences between static and flexible budget variances.
*   Develop budget revisions based on historical results.
*   Identify overhead costs by their behavior over increasing volume.
*   Alter the worksheet to include an additional overhead cost.
*   Create a chart contrasting the budget variances of the static and flexible budgets.

PROBLEM DATA

Sampson Clock Works has just completed an in-depth study of overhead costs. The firm normally operates between 3,600 and 4,600 labor hours each month. Budgeted costs for this range of activity are presented below:

Depreciation	$4,000
Maintenance	$1,800 plus $0.70 per direct labor hour
Indirect labor	$2,800 plus $0.25 per direct labor hour
Utilities	$4,000 plus $0.20 per direct labor hour
Indirect material	$0.25 per direct labor hour
Overtime	$2.25 for each direct labor hour in excess of 4,000 direct labor hours per month

During April, Sampson had planned to operate at 4,500 direct labor hours. Actual activity amounted to only 4,100 hours with the following costs:

Depreciation	$4,000
Maintenance	4,730
Indirect labor	4,240
Utilities	4,900
Indirect material	1,125
Overtime	260

All fixed cost elements remained as budgeted.

REQUIRED

1. The president of the company has asked you to analyze the overhead costs in April by preparing a report making comparisons of actual costs to the original (static) budget which was prepared using the budget data presented. The vice president of operations is interested in a similar report, but one that utilizes flexible budgeting concepts. The work-sheet called FLEXBUD that follows these requirements has been provided for your assistance. Note that the initial problem data is already entered in the Data Section of the worksheet.

2. Using the spaces provided below, enter the 12 formulas required to complete the work-sheet. FORMULA6 and FORMULA12 will utilize the =IF function discussed in Appendix A of *Excel Quick*.

   FORMULA1_____   FORMULA7_____

   FORMULA2_____   FORMULA8_____

   FORMULA3_____   FORMULA9_____

   FORMULA4_____   FORMULA10_____

   FORMULA5_____   FORMULA11_____

   FORMULA6_____   FORMULA12_____

3. Start the spreadsheet program and open the file FLEXBUD from the Student Disk. Enter the 12 formulas in the appropriate cells. Enter your name in cell A1. Save your results as FLEXBUD3 and print the worksheet when done. Also print your formulas. *Check figure: Total flexible budget difference (cell E43), $690 unfavorable.*

4. Comment on the differences between the static and flexible budget performance reports. Which budget is more useful in appraising the performance of the various persons charged with the responsibility for cost control? Why?

WHAT-IF ANALYSIS

5.   The following actual overhead costs were incurred in May:

Depreciation	$4,000
Maintenance	5,150
Indirect labor	4,420
Utilities	4,900
Indirect material	1,350
Overtime	1,125

Planned direct labor hours were 4,000. Actual direct labor hours were 4,500. Other budget data for May were identical to April except that fixed maintenance costs have increased to $2,000 and variable indirect materials costs have increased to $0.30 per direct labor hour.

Prepare and print new budget reports for May. Remember to change the month in cell B7. Save your completed file as FLEXBUD5. Compare the two budget reports and comment on the differences disclosed between the static budget and flexible budget performance reports.

6.   If you were to suggest a revision to the budget for May, which cost category seems most in need of revision? Assuming that the fixed cost component of this budgeted cost is already correct, what should the variable cost component be so that the budget equals actual? Try different values in the appropriate cell in the Data Section and write your answer below.

CHART ANALYSIS

7.   Click the Chart sheet tab. On the chart, lines are plotting the cost behavior patterns of four of the overhead costs from this problem. Examine the patterns, review the Data Section, and identify below which of the four costs each represents.

A_____

B_____

C_____

D_____

When the assignment is complete, close the file without saving it again.

TICKLERS (optional)

Worksheet. The controller of Sampson Clock Works has discovered that insurance costs were mistakenly omitted from the FLEXBUD3 worksheet. Insert new lines for insurance costs (right under maintenance costs) and redo the April performance reports to include the following information about insurance costs:

Budget: $1,200 per month plus $0.35 per direct labor hour
Actual: $2,500

Use the Print Preview command (File menu) to make sure that the worksheet will print neatly on one page, then print the worksheet. Save the completed file as FLEXBUDT.

Chart. Using the FLEXBUD3 file, prepare a column chart which graphically represents the budget variances shown on both budgets. No Chart Data Table is needed. Use A28 to A33 as the X-axis. Use E28 to E33 and E37 to E42 as the two data ranges. Use appropriate titles, legends, formats, etc. Put your name somewhere on the chart. Save the file again as FLEXBUD3. Print the chart.

	A	B	C	D	E
2			FLEXBUD		
3			Flexible Budgeting		
4					
5	Data Section				
6					
7	For the month of:		April		
8					
9			Budget Data		
10		Fixed	Variable		Actual
11		Portion	Portion*		Data
12	Depreciation	$4,000	--		$4,000
13	Maintenance	$1,800	$0.70		4,730
14	Indirect labor	$2,800	0.25		4,240
15	Utilities	$4,000	0.20		4,900
16	Indirect material		0.25		1,125
17	Overtime		2.25 **		260
18					
19		*per direct labor hour			
20		**per monthly direct labor hours in excess of			4,000
21					
22		Planned direct labor hours for the month			4,500
23		Actual direct labor hours for the month			4,100
24					
25	Answer Section				
26					
27	Static Budget		Budget	Actual	Difference
28	Depreciation		FORMULA1	$0	$0
29	Maintenance		FORMULA2	0	0
30	Indirect labor		FORMULA3	0	0
31	Utilities		FORMULA4	0	0
32	Indirect material		FORMULA5	0	0
33	Overtime		FORMULA6	0	0
34			$0	$0	$0
35					
36	Flexible Budget		Budget	Actual	Difference
37	Depreciation		FORMULA7	$0	$0
38	Maintenance		FORMULA8	0	0
39	Indirect labor		FORMULA9	0	0
40	Utilities		FORMULA10	0	0
41	Indirect material		FORMULA11	0	0
42	Overtime		FORMULA12	0	0
43			$0	$0	$0
44					

P24 ♦ MATERIAL AND LABOR VARIANCES (PRIMEVAR)

LEARNING OBJECTIVES

• Calculate materials price and quantity variances; calculate labor rate and efficiency variances; automatically label variances as being favorable or unfavorable.
• Interpret cost data to determine proper inputs for variance analysis.
• Interpret variances for management implications.
• Alter the worksheet to include overhead variance analysis (2-, 3-, or 4-way).
• Create a chart comparing standard unit costs with actual unit costs.

PROBLEM DATA

Mark Industries manufactures a product whose standard direct materials and direct labor unit costs are as follows:

Direct materials: 5 pounds at $16 per pound	$80
Direct labor: 6 hours at $8 per hour	48

Actual data for October:
    Actual production: 7,600 units
Direct materials used in production: 39,500 pounds costing $628,050
Direct labor: 44,000 hours costing $354,200

REQUIRED

1. What is the total actual cost of October's production? Based on the standards, what should it have cost? Compute the total difference (variance) between these two amounts.

2. The president of Mark Industries wants an analysis prepared to help explain why the variance computed in requirement 1 occurred. Using the worksheet called PRIMEVAR that follows these requirements, calculate the material and labor variances for Mark Industries. The problem requires you to enter the input in the Data Section, as well as formulas in the Answer Section.

3. Use the problem data to determine the values (or formulas) to be entered as INPUT A, INPUT B, etc., in the Data Section of the worksheet. For now, pencil them in on the printout of PRIMEVAR.

4. In the spaces provided below, write the formulas requested in the worksheet. FORMULA1 has been done for you as an example. Formulas 8–10 should enter an F if the variance is favorable and a U if it is unfavorable. See the discussion of the =IF function in Appendix A of *Excel Quick*.

FORMULA1_____=(D8-D9)*D12_____   FORMULA6_____

FORMULA2_____   FORMULA7_____

FORMULA3_____   FORMULA8_____

FORMULA4_____   FORMULA9_____

FORMULA5_____   FORMULA10_____

5. Start the spreadsheet program and open the file PRIMEVAR from the Student Disk. Enter the input values or formulas to compute the input values. Then enter the formulas where indicated on the worksheet. Enter your name in cell A1. Save the completed file as PRIMEVA5. Print the worksheet when done. Also print your formulas. *Check figure: Material quantity variance (cell B27), $24,000 U.*

WHAT-IF ANALYSIS

6. The worksheet you have developed will handle most simple variance analysis problems. Try the problem below for KPW, Inc.:

| | Cost Per Unit | |
	Standard	Actual
Direct materials:		
Standard: 1.25 pounds at $10 per pound	$12.50	
Actual: 1.20 pounds at $10.50 per pound		$12.60
Direct labor:		
Standard: 3.5 hours at $6.00 per hour	21.00	
Actual: 4 hours at $5.85 per hour		23.40

Actual production for October was 11,500 units. Compute the direct materials and direct labor variances for KPW, Inc. Be careful when entering your input because this problem presents the information in a different format from the Mark Industries' data. Save the file as PRIMEVA6. Print the worksheet when done.

CHART ANALYSIS

7.   Close the PRIMEVA6 file and open PRIMEVA5. Click the Chart sheet tab. On the screen is a graphical representation of the variances computed in requirement 5. Review the chart and answer the following questions:

a.   Which variances does each bar represent?

A

B

C

D

b.   Which of the variances shown would be of most concern to management for immediate attention? (Consider groups of variances and materiality also.) Explain.

When the assignment is complete, close the file without saving it again.

TICKLERS (optional)

Worksheet. Mark Industries also has the following information regarding overhead for October: actual overhead $375,000, standard variable overhead of $3 per direct labor hour, and standard fixed overhead of $5 per direct labor hour (based on 47,000 hours budgeted). Modify the PRIMEVA5 worksheet to compute all appropriate overhead variances. Use the Print Preview command (File menu) to make sure that the worksheet will print neatly on one page, then print the worksheet. Save the completed file as PRIMEVAT.

Hint: Insert several new rows in the Data Section and in the Answer Section.

Chart. Using the PRIMEVA5 file, prepare a 3-D stacked bar chart to compare total standard cost per unit with actual cost per unit. Complete the Chart Tickler Data Table and use it as a basis for preparing the chart. You do not need to use cell references when completing the table. Enter all appropriate titles, legends, and formats. Put your name somewhere on the chart. Save the file again as PRIMEVA5. Print the chart.

	A	B	C	D
2	*PRIMEVAR*			
3	*Material and Labor Variances*			
4				
5	Data Section			
6				
7	Materials price variance input			
8	Actual cost of material per pound (ounce, etc.)			INPUT A
9	Standard cost of mat. per pound (ounce, etc.)			INPUT B
10				
11	Materials quantity variance input			
12	Actual quantity of materials used			INPUT C
13	Standard quantity of mat. used for actual output			INPUT D
14				
15	Labor rate variance input			
16	Actual cost of labor per hour			INPUT E
17	Standard cost of labor per hour			INPUT F
18				
19	Labor efficiency variance input			
20	Actual quantity of hours incurred			INPUT G
21	Standard quantity of hours for actual output			INPUT H
22				
23	Answer Section			
24				
25				F or U
26	Material price variance	FORMULA1		FORMULA8
27	Material quantity variance	FORMULA2		FORMULA9
28				
29	Total materials variance		FORMULA3	FORMULA10
30				
31	Labor rate variance	FORMULA4		N/A
32	Labor efficiency variance	FORMULA5		N/A
33				
34	Total labor variance		FORMULA6	N/A
35				
36	Total materials and labor variances		FORMULA7	N/A
37				

P25 ◆ SEGMENT INCOME STATEMENT (DEPT)

LEARNING OBJECTIVES

- Develop departmental income statements using various cost allocation bases.
- Assess departmental performance using the cost allocation bases.
- Alter the worksheet to determine whether a department should be eliminated; utilize departmental contribution margin and indirect expense analysis.
- Create two charts showing the expense composition of two departments.

PROBLEM DATA

Forked Creek Bungee Supply Inc. has divided its operations into two departments: Supplies, devoted to selling bungee cords and supplies; and Apparel, devoted to selling sports clothing and some bungee wear. Departmental expense accounts are kept for direct expenses, but indirect (common) expenses are not allocated until the end of the accounting period. Selected data at June 30, 2004, the end of the current fiscal year, are as follows:

	Apparel	Supplies	Indirect Expenses
Departmental operating expenses:			
Sales salaries	$18,000	$30,000	
Rent			$19,000
Administrative salaries			25,000
Advertising	3,000	2,000	800
Supplies used	1,175	1,625	
Payroll taxes (12% of salaries)			8,760
Insurance expense			6,400
Depreciation expense	300	350	
Miscellaneous expense	325	220	200
	$22,800	$34,195	$60,160

	Apparel	Supplies	Totals
Other departmental data:			
Net sales	$69,000	$160,000	$229,000
Cost of goods sold	24,000	55,000	79,000
Average inventory	17,000	19,000	36,000
Floor space (square feet)	800	800	1,600
Fixtures (original cost)	2,740	3,260	6,000

The bases for allocating indirect expenses are as follows:

Indirect Expense	Basis of Allocation
Rent	Floor space
Administrative salaries	Gross profit
Advertising	Net sales
Payroll taxes	Direct and indirect salaries
Insurance expense	Sum of fixtures and average inventory
Miscellaneous expense	Supplies used

REQUIRED

1. As the accountant for Forked Creek Bungee Supply, you have been asked to prepare a departmental income statement. Review the worksheet DEPT that follows these requirements. All of the problem information relating to direct expenses has been entered into the Answer Section. You will be allocating the indirect expenses to the appropriate departments.

2. In the spaces provided below, write the formulas requested. FORMULA1 has been provided for you as an example.

FORMULA1 _____=(B20/D20)*B8_____   FORMULA6_____

FORMULA2_____   FORMULA7_____

FORMULA3_____   FORMULA8_____

FORMULA4_____   FORMULA9_____

FORMULA5_____   FORMULA10_____

3. Start the spreadsheet program and open the file DEPT from the Student Disk. Enter the formulas where indicated on the worksheet. The cells that contain zeros now have been pre-programmed. They will change to non-zero values as the formulas are entered. Enter your name in cell A1. Save your file as DEPT3. Print the worksheet when done. Also print your formulas. *Check figure: Operating income, Supplies department (cell C47), $34,038.*

4. What conclusions can be drawn from this departmental income statement?

WHAT-IF ANALYSIS

5. The sales manager for the Apparel department maintains that rent should be allocated on the basis of net sales rather than on floor space. The manager thinks this is fairer since the Supplies department occupies more "prime location" floor space than does the Apparel department. Alter FORMULA1 and FORMULA2 (cells B40 and C40, respectively) on the worksheet to see what effect this "fairer" allocation would have on each department's operating income. Save the revision as DEPT5. Print the worksheet when done.

6. Comment on the results of this change and on the appropriateness of the new allocation scheme.

CHART ANALYSIS

7. The sales manager of the Apparel department feels she has her direct expenses under control, but she is still concerned with the amount of indirect expenses allocated to her department. She has prepared a chart showing the percentage of sales made by her department and the percentage of expenses incurred. Open DEPT3 and click the Chart sheet tab. Then open DEPT5 and click the Chart sheet tab. Is her concern warranted? Explain.

When the assignment is complete, close the file without saving it again.

TICKLERS (optional)

Worksheet. The president of Forked Creek is considering whether the Apparel department should be eliminated. She wants to see departmental income statements that show each department's contribution toward indirect expenses. Modify the DEPT3 worksheet so that it can help her with this decision. Use the Print Preview command (File menu) to make sure that the worksheet will print neatly on one page, then print the worksheet. Save the revision as DEPTT. Should the Apparel department be eliminated? Explain.

Hint: Insert rows and formulas to subtotal the direct expenses. Use these amounts to determine departmental contribution. Do not allocate the indirect expenses (i.e., erase all allocation formulas and redo the formulas in the total column).

Chart. Using the DEPT3 file, prepare two pie charts, one of which shows the composition of expenses for the Apparel department (cost of goods sold, total direct expenses, and total allocated indirect expenses), and the other for the Supplies department. Complete the Chart Tickler Data Table and use it as a basis for preparing each chart. Enter an appropriate title for each. Put your name somewhere on each chart. Save the file again as DEPT3. Print both charts.

	A	B	C	D
2		DEPT		
3		Segment Income Statement		
4				
5	Data Section			
6				
7	Indirect Expenses			
8	Rent	$19,000		
9	Administrative salaries	25,000		
10	Advertising	800		
11	Payroll taxes	8,760		
12	Insurance expense	6,400		
13	Miscellaneous expense	200		
14				
15	Other Departmental Expenses			
16		Apparel	Supplies	Totals
17	Net sales	$69,000	$160,000	$229,000
18	Cost of goods sold	24,000	55,000	79,000
19	Average inventory	17,000	19,000	36,000
20	Floor space (square feet)	800	800	1,600
21	Fixtures (original cost)	2,740	3,260	6,000
22				
23	Answer Section			
24				
25	Forked Creek Bungee Supply Inc.			
26	Departmental Income Statement			
27	June 30, 2004			
28				
29				
30		Apparel	Supplies	Totals
31	Net sales	$69,000	$160,000	$229,000
32	Cost of goods sold	24,000	55,000	79,000
33	Gross profit	$45,000	$105,000	$150,000
34	Operating expenses:			
35	Sales salaries	$18,000	$30,000	$48,000
36	Advertising (direct)	3,000	2,000	5,000
37	Supplies used	1,175	1,625	2,800
38	Depreciation on equipment	300	350	650
39	Miscellaneous expense (direct)	325	220	545
40	Rent	FORMULA1	FORMULA2	FORMULA3
41	Administrative salaries	FORMULA4	FORMULA5	FORMULA6
42	Advertising (indirect)	FORMULA7	0	0
43	Payroll taxes	FORMULA8	0	0
44	Insurance expense	0	FORMULA9	0
45	Miscellaneous expenses (indirect)	0	FORMULA10	0
46	Total operating expenses	$0	$0	$0
47	Operating income	$0	$0	$0
48				

P26 ♦ CAPITAL BUDGETING (CAPBUD)

LEARNING OBJECTIVES

• Evaluate capital investment projects using payback period, accounting rate of return, net present value analysis, and internal rate of return using the =NPV and =IRR functions.
• Perform sensitivity analysis on cost, salvage value, and annual cash flows.
• Interpret investment data to determine proper inputs to capital budgeting decisions.
• Alter the worksheet to include projects with uneven cash flows.
• Create a chart showing the sensitivity of net present value to changes in the cost of the investment.

PROBLEM DATA

Musk Interiors, a chain of exclusive furniture stores, is considering renting space in a new shopping mall. It is anticipated that this rental will require an investment in fixtures and equipment costing $190,000, with an estimated salvage value of $10,000 at the end of its useful life in 10 years. The new store is expected to generate annual net cash flow of $40,000. The owner desires a 20% annual return on investment and wants a payback period of less than four years. Ignore the impact of taxes.

REQUIRED

1. Use the worksheet called CAPBUD that follows these requirements to evaluate this investment. Note that the investment information is already entered in the Data Section of the worksheet. Note also that there is a scratch pad at the bottom of the worksheet. The numbers in the scratch pad are needed as input to the net present value and internal rate of return calculations.

2. In the spaces provided below, enter the four formulas requested. Carefully review Appendix A in *Excel Quick* for instructions on using the =NPV and =IRR functions.

    FORMULA1_____   FORMULA3_____

    FORMULA2_____   FORMULA4_____

3. Start the spreadsheet program and open the file CAPBUD from the Student Disk. Enter the above formulas. Enter your name in cell A1. Save the results as CAPBUD3 and print the worksheet when done. Also print your formulas. *Check figure: Internal rate of return (cell E18), 16.78%.*

4. Should Musk Interiors make the investment in the new store? Explain.

WHAT-IF ANALYSIS

5. Musk Interiors would like to test the sensitivity of the estimates used for the input data to compute the net present value and internal rate of return on this investment. Ignore the payback period and the accounting rate of return. Consider a, b, and c below independently by holding everything else constant:

    a. What is the minimum cost of the investment (to the nearest $100) needed for the owner to accept it?

    b. Reset cost to $190,000. What is the minimum salvage value (to the nearest $100) needed for the owner to accept it?

    c. Reset salvage value to $10,000. What is the minimum annual cash flow (to the nearest $100) needed for the owner to accept it?

    Comment on the results of these analyses. How sensitive is the decision to accept or reject this investment to the estimates used for input data?

6. Musk Interiors is also considering introducing a computerized interior design service. The company will have to spend $37,000 for equipment, $3,000 for installation, and $8,000 for testing. The equipment will have no salvage value at the end of four years. Estimated annual results for the project are:

Service fees		$53,000
Expenses other than depreciation	$33,000	
Depreciation (straight-line)	12,000	45,000
Net income		$ 8,000

    Enter the new information in the Data Section. Assuming the criteria for accepting a project have not changed, should Musk Interiors invest in this service? Explain. Print the worksheet when done.

CHART ANALYSIS

7. Reset the Data Section of the CAPBUD3 worksheet to the original values. In requirement 5, you assessed the sensitivity of the investment's internal rate of return to changes in some of the input data. This was done in a trial-and-error fashion. Click the Chart sheet tab. Presented on the screen is a graphical analysis of the sensitivity of the internal rate of return to changes in annual cash flows. To demonstrate the usefulness of such a chart, note the ease

with which you are able to answer the following questions that might be of interest to the owner:

a. What annual cash flow (approximately) is required to:
    1) Earn 0% rate of return?_____
    2) Earn 20% rate of return?_____
    3) Earn over 30% rate of return?_____
    4) Earn between 10% and 20% rate of return?_____

b. Approximately, how much is the rate of return reduced for each drop of $10,000 annual cash flow?

When the assignment is complete, close the file without saving it again.

TICKLERS (optional)

Worksheet. The CAPBUD3 worksheet handles only cash inflows that are even in amount each year. Many capital projects generate uneven cash inflows. Suppose that the new store had expected cash earnings of $20,000 per year for the first two years, $35,000 for the next four years, and $55,000 for the last four years. The new store will generate the same total cash return ($400,000) as in the original problem, but the timing of the cash flows is different. Alter the CAPBUD3 worksheet so that the NPV and IRR calculations can be made whether there are even or uneven cash flows. When done, use the Print Preview command (File menu) to make sure that the worksheet will print neatly on one page, then print the worksheet. Save the completed file as CAPBUDT.

Hint: One suggestion is to label column F in the scratch pad as Uneven Cash Flows. Enter the uneven cash flows for each year. Modify FORMULA3 to include these cash flows. Modify the formulas in the range E30 to E39 to include the new data. Then set cell E10 (estimated Annual Net Cash Inflow) to zero. When you have even cash flows, use cell E10 and set column F in the scratch pad to zeros. If you have uneven cash flows, set cell E10 to zero and fill in column F in the scratch pad.

Note that this solution causes garbage to come out in cells E15 and E16 because those formulas were not altered. *Check figure for uneven cash flows: NPV cell E17, ($47,226).*

Chart. Using the CAPBUD3 file, develop a chart just like the one used in requirement 7 to show the sensitivity of net present value to changes in cost of the investment amount from $160,000 to $190,000 (use $5,000 increments). Complete the Chart Tickler Data Table and use it as a basis for preparing the chart. Put your name somewhere on the chart. Save the file again as CAPBUD3. Print the chart.

	A	B	C	D	E	F
2	CAPBUD					
3	Capital Budgeting					
4						
5	Data Section					
6						
7	Cost of investment (initial outlay)				$190,000	
8	Estimated life of investment				10	years
9	Estimated salvage value				$10,000	
10	Estimated annual net cash inflow				$40,000	
11	Required rate of return				20.00%	
12						
13	Answer Section					
14						
15	Payback period				FORMULA1	years
16	Accounting (average) rate of return				FORMULA2	
17	Net present value				FORMULA3	
18	Internal rate of return				FORMULA4	
19						
20						
21						
22						
23			Scratch Pad			
24			Cash flow table needed for			
25			NPV & IRR calculations			
26			NPV		IRR	
27			Annual	Salvage	Combined	
28		Year	Cash Flow	Value	Flows	
29		0			-190000	
30		1	40000	0	40000	
31		2	40000	0	40000	
32		3	40000	0	40000	
33		4	40000	0	40000	
34		5	40000	0	40000	
35		6	40000	0	40000	
36		7	40000	0	40000	
37		8	40000	0	40000	
38		9	40000	0	40000	
39		10	40000	10000	50000	
40						

MODEL-BUILDING PROBLEM CHECKLIST

Before submitting any model-building solution to your instructor, review the following list to ensure that your worksheet is presented in a clear, concise manner.

1. Enter your name in cell A1 and the name of the file in cell A2. (Use the file name given in the problem.)

2. Include the name of the company, the name of the statement or schedule presented, and the date (e.g., 2005, 4th Quarter, June). The date should be in an unprotected cell.

3. Use cell references in your formulas wherever possible.

4. Format all cells properly. Place dollar signs ($) at the top of all amount columns and below all subtotal rules.

5. Use zero decimal places whenever decimal accuracy is not required. Generally, if the problem statement does not include cents, your answer will not require cents.

6. Vary column widths to fit the data presented.

7. Place titles at the top of all data columns (one exception is on financial statements where the statement heading is sufficient). Titles should be centered or right justified in the columns.

8. Use Data Sections wherever appropriate. If a Data Section is used, it should be labeled as such.

9. Use file protection where appropriate on the worksheet. Unprotect the cells where changeable data or labels are to be entered.

10. Use upper and lowercase letters as appropriate. Generally uppercase letters are needed as the first letter in all headings and titles.

11. Use the =ROUND function to eliminate rounding discrepancies.

12. Printouts should include no unusual spacing or gaps in the middle of the page. Wide worksheets should be printed using landscape orientation. Use the Size option "Fit all to page" to reduce printouts to a single page if at all possible.

M1 ◆ TRIAL BALANCE

Note: For a problem using the corporate form of business organization, download FTB from http://smith.swlearning.com.

The general ledger of Joshua Tree Consulting shows the following balances at September 30:

Cash	$22,548
Accounts receivable	13,004
Supplies on hand	5,425
Accounts payable	2,228
Salaries payable	4,565
Stormy Kromer, capital	40,134
Stormy Kromer, drawing	12,000
Consulting fees	25,625
Rent expense	2,000
Salary expense	14,090
Supplies expense	2,775
Utilities expense	550
Miscellaneous expense	160

Kromer has asked you to develop a worksheet that will serve as a trial balance (file name PTB). Use the data above as input for your model.

Review the Model-Building Problem Checklist on page 173 to ensure that your worksheet is complete. Print the worksheet when done. *Check figure: Total debits, $72,552.*

To test your model, use the following balances at October 31:

Cash	$26,422
Accounts receivable	11,810
Supplies on hand	4,266
Accounts payable	1,495
Salaries payable	4,656
Stormy Kromer, capital	34,184
Stormy Kromer, drawing	13,500
Consulting fees	32,805
Rent expense	2,000
Salary expense	12,330
Supplies expense	2,022
Utilities expense	605
Miscellaneous expense	185

Print the worksheet when done. *Check figure: Total debits, $73,140.*

CHART (optional)

Using the test data worksheet, prepare a pie chart showing the percentage of each asset to total assets. Print the chart when done.

M2 ♦ SERVICE COMPANY FINANCIAL STATEMENTS

Note: For a problem using the sole proprietorship form of business organization, download PFS from http://smith.swlearning.com.

The ledger of Knickerbocker Corp. showed the following balances after adjustment on June 30, 2004, the end of the current fiscal year:

Accounts payable	$ 75,600	General expenses	$112,350
Accounts receivable	103,890	Interest expense	6,750
Accumulated depreciation—		Merchandise inventory	157,500
equipment	26,250	Notes payable	46,335
Cash	80,370	Prepaid insurance	10,125
Common stock	300,000	Retained earnings,	
Cost of merchandise sold	621,450	July 1, 2003	0
Dividends	18,000	Sales	943,500
Equipment	142,500	Selling expenses	138,750

The president of Knickerbocker has asked you to develop a financial statement worksheet (file name PFS) that includes a single-step income statement, a statement of retained earnings, and a balance sheet. This worksheet will allow the financial statements to be prepared quickly by entering account balances in the appropriate cells on the worksheet. Use the information above as input for your worksheet.

Review the Model-Building Problem Checklist on page 173 to ensure that your worksheet is complete. Print the worksheet when done. *Check figure: Total assets, $468,135.*

To test your model, use the following data for the year ended June 30, 2005:

Accounts payable	$ 67,050	General expenses	$108,150
Accounts receivable	92,700	Interest expense	9,000
Accumulated depreciation—		Merchandise inventory	120,750
equipment	52,500	Notes payable	44,085
Cash	97,650	Prepaid insurance	10,800
Common stock	300,000	Retained earnings,	
Cost of merchandise sold	659,835	July 1, 2004	46,200
Dividends	27,000	Sales	892,500
Equipment	147,000	Selling expenses	129,450

Print the worksheet when done. *Check figure: Total assets, $416,400.*

CHART (optional)

Utilizing the test data worksheet, prepare a pie chart depicting the percentage of each expense (including cost of merchandising sold) to total expenses. Print the chart when done.

M3 ◆ CASH RECEIPTS JOURNAL

The terms of sales on account offered by Gordon's General Store are 2/10, n/30. During the first week of March, the following transactions involved receiving cash:

March 1 Received $793.80 from Seaton Inc. in payment of a February 22 invoice of $810, less discount.
3 Received a loan of $4,500 from First National Bank.
4 Received $558.25 from King World in payment of a February 23 invoice.
5 Received $721.28 from Wagner Corp. in payment of a February 28 invoice of $736, less discount.
7 Cash sales for the week totaled $9,500.

Gordon's General Store has asked you to create a computerized cash receipts journal (file name CRJ). The journal should include one column each for the Date, Account Name, Other Accounts Cr., Sales Cr., Accounts Receivable Cr., Sales Discount Dr., and Cash Dr. The appropriate columns should be totaled. Use the data for the first week in March as input for the worksheet.

Review the Model-Building Problem Checklist on page 173 to ensure that your worksheet is complete. Print the worksheet when done. *Check figure: Total debits, $16,104.25.*

To test your model, use the following information for the second week of March:

March 8 Received $426.30 from XYZ Inc. in payment of a March 1 invoice of $435, less discount.
9 Received $896.70 from King World in payment of a February 28 invoice of $915, less discount.
12 Received $712.75 from Ives Stores in payment of a March 1 invoice.
13 Received $150 for old store equipment that had no book value.
14 Cash sales for the week totaled $9,000.

Print the worksheet when done. *Check figure: Total debits, $11,212.75.*

CHART (optional)

Using your test model, create a 3-D column chart showing the amount of cash Gordon's General Store collected from each customer the second week of March. Print the chart when done.

M4 ◆ SHORT-TERM INVESTMENTS

Parkway Products has the following portfolio of trading securities at December 31, 2004. All shares were purchased during 2004.

	Shares Held at 12/31/04	Cost Per Share	Market Value Per Share
Grand Corp. shares	150	$ 25.13	$ 32.50
Lenor Inc. shares	600	58.00	55.73
Yeager Co. shares	500	34.25	29.00
Pentwater Inc. shares	100	112.87	108.44

Develop a worksheet (file name STI) that will automatically compute the total cost of stock in the portfolio and the total market value. The worksheet should also disclose the value of the portfolio to be shown on the December 31, 2004, balance sheet. Use the above data as input for your model.

Review the Model-Building Problem Checklist on page 173 to ensure that your worksheet is complete. Print the worksheet when done. *Check figure: Balance sheet value at 12/31/04, $63,657.00.* Extra assignment: Prepare the adjusting journal entry required at 12/31/04.

Use the following 12/31/05 market value to test your model:

	Market Value Per Share
Grand Corp.	$ 28.32
Lenor Inc.	60.75
Yeager Co.	35.47
Pentwater Inc.	101.01

Print the worksheet when done. *Check figure: Balance sheet value at 12/31/05, $68,534.00.* Extra assignment: Prepare the adjusting journal entry required at 12/31/05.

CHART (optional)

Using the test model, prepare a pie graph showing the percentage that the market value for each security is of the total portfolio. Print the chart when done.

M5 ◆ PERPETUAL INVENTORY RECORD

Beginning inventory, purchases, and sales data for Part Number 47B-2 are presented below. A perpetual inventory account is maintained for this part using the weighted-average costing method. Develop a worksheet (file name PERPTL) to be used as a perpetual inventory record for this part. Your worksheet should include columns for date, quantity purchased, total cost of units purchased, quantity sold, total cost of units sold, quantity balance, total cost balance, and weighted-average unit cost.

April	1	Inventory	22 units costing $550 in total
	5	Sold	10 units
	12	Purchased	15 units costing $380 in total
	18	Sold	13 units
	25	Sold	5 units
	29	Purchased	20 units costing $505 in total

Review the Model-Building Problem Checklist on page 173 to ensure that your worksheet is complete. Print the worksheet when done. *Check figure: Ending inventory balance, $731.67.*

To test your model, record the following transactions for May:

May	1	Inventory	29 units costing $731.67 in total
	7	Purchased	20 units costing $511 in total
	11	Sold	12 units
	22	Sold	22 units
	30	Purchased	20 units costing $518 in total

Print the worksheet when done. *Check figure: Ending inventory balance, $898.41.*

CHART (optional)

Create a line chart on the test data template showing the trend in weighted-average prices after each purchase over the two-month period.

M6 ◆ INVENTORY VALUATION: LOWER OF COST OR MARKET

Information about Land of Sleep's inventory at June 30, is as follows:

Mattress	Inventory Quantity	Unit Cost	Unit Market
Queen	75	$240	$235
King	165	310	330
Double	43	150	155
Twin	120	105	90

You have been asked to develop a worksheet that will determine the value of the inventory on an item-by-item basis at the lower of cost or market value (file name LCOM). You should find it helpful to use the =MIN function discussed in Appendix A of *Excel Quick*. Use the data above as input for your worksheet.

Review the Model-Building Problem Checklist on page 173 to ensure that your worksheet is complete. Print the worksheet when done. *Check figure: Lower of cost or market inventory value, $86,025.*

To test your model, use the following information about Land of Sleep's inventory at September 30:

Mattress	Inventory Quantity	Unit Cost	Unit Market
Queen	90	$240	$245
King	145	310	315
Double	45	150	145
Twin	160	105	100

Print the worksheet when done. *Check figure: Lower of cost or market inventory value, $89,075.*

CHART (optional)

From the test data worksheet, design a 3-D column chart demonstrating the relationship between total cost and total market value for each commodity. Print the chart when done.

M7 ♦ LUMP SUM PURCHASE

Taylor Management owns several apartment complexes throughout the city of Cincinnati. They just acquired a new piece of property that has been appraised at $1,600,000. The assets and their values are listed below.

Asset	Value
Building	$ 700,000
Equipment	200,000
Furniture	100,000
Land	500,000
Land Improvements	100,000
	$ 1,600,000

Taylor Management purchased the property for $1,000,000. Create a worksheet (file name BASKET) that will allocate the purchase price among the assets acquired.

Review the Model-Building Problem Checklist on page 173 to ensure that your worksheet is complete. Print the worksheet when done. *Check figure: Allocated cost of the building, $437,500.*

Use the following purchase price to test your model: $1,200,000.

Print the worksheet when done. *Check figure: Allocated cost of the building at the purchase price of $1,200,000, $525,000.*

CHART (optional)

Using the data template, prepare a pie chart that shows the percentage that each asset is of the total appraised value. Print the chart when done.

M8 ♦ BONDS VS. STOCK FINANCING

Gator Corporation is considering different methods of financing a $600,000 expansion of plant facilities. At present, there are 70,000 shares of $20 par common stock outstanding. One financing plan under consideration calls for issuing an additional 20,000 shares of $20 par common stock at $25 per share and $100,000 of 10-year, 10% bonds at face value. The president has asked you to develop a worksheet that will calculate expected earnings per share (file name NEWMONEY) if this financing plan is adopted. Your worksheet should include a Data Section. Net income before bond interest is expected to be $1,000,000. Assume an income tax rate of 40%.

Review the Model-Building Problem Checklist on page 173 to ensure that your worksheet is complete. Print the worksheet when done. *Check figure: Earnings per share, $6.60.*

To test your model, calculate expected earnings per share if $600,000 of 10-year, 10% bonds are issued at face value and no new shares of stock are issued. *Check figure: Earnings per share, $8.06.*

CHART (optional)

Using the test data worksheet, create a line chart to show the trend in earnings per share as the portion of bond financing changes from $0 to $600,000. Use $200,000 increments. Assume that the total to be financed is $600,000 and that common stock (at $25 per share) will be issued to cover any amount not financed by bonds. Print the chart.

M9 ♦ PARTNERSHIP: DIVISION OF NET INCOME

Missy and Leah recently formed a partnership called Erie East Salon. Missy invested $30,000 cash, and Leah invested $30,000 of plant assets and $15,000 cash. The partners are trying to find an equitable way of splitting the income to take into account that Leah invested more capital, but Missy will spend twice as much time as Leah in running the business. They have asked you to develop a worksheet (file name PSHIP) to allow them to see the effect of:

- Various interest rates on invested capital
- Various salary allowances for time spent
- Various levels of partnership net income

The easiest way to achieve this flexibility is to use a Data Section. Use the following information as input for your model:

Net income	$75,000
Division of net income:	
Interest on original investments at 15%	
Salary allowances:	
Missy	60,000
Leah	30,000
Remainder shared equally	

Review the Model-Building Problem Checklist on page 173 to ensure that your worksheet is complete. Print the worksheet when done. *Check figure: Missy's share of income, $51,375.*

To test your model, use the following profit-sharing scenario:

Net income	$125,000
Division of net income:	
Interest on original investments at 10%	
Salary allowances:	
Missy	50,000
Leah	25,000
Remainder shared equally	

Print the worksheet when done. *Check figure: Missy's share of income, $74,250.*

CHART (optional)

Using the test data provided, prepare a 3-D stacked column chart showing the division of net income (salary, interest, and remainder) to each partner. Print the chart when done.

M10 ♦ CORPORATE INCOME STATEMENT

The following data were selected from the records of Parma Incorporated for the month ended January 31:

Advertising expense	$12,300	Insurance expense	$ 500
Depreciation expense—		Interest expense	2,500
office equipment	500	Loss from disposal of a	
Depreciation expense—store		segment of business	23,000
equipment	2,500	Merchandise inventory, January 1	75,000
Extraordinary loss	10,000	Merchandise inventory, January 31	68,000
Income tax:		Office salaries expense	17,000
On continuing operations	15,000	Office supplies expense	1,025
Reduction applicable to loss		Purchases	300,000
from disposal of a segment		Rent expense	500
of the business	4,500	Sales	425,500
Reduction applicable to		Sales salaries expense	15,000
extraordinary loss	1,200	Store supplies expense	2,525

This firm's accounting system generates these totals on a monthly basis. You have been asked to develop a worksheet (file name IS) that will allow a monthly income statement to be prepared by entering monthly figures in the appropriate cells. The income statement should include a section for earnings per share. There were 20,000 shares of common stock (no preferred) outstanding throughout the month. Use the data above as input for your worksheet.

Review the Model-Building Problem Checklist on page 173 to ensure that your worksheet is complete. Print the worksheet when done. *Check figure: January net income, $21,850.*

To test your model, use the following data for the month ended February 28:

Advertising expense	$11,500	Insurance expense	$ 500
Depreciation expense—		Interest expense	6,000
office equipment	810	Loss from disposal of a segment	
Depreciation expense—		of business (additional ex-	
store equipment	3,235	penses from January disposal)	1,000
Extraordinary loss (additional		Merchandise inventory, February 1	68,000
expenses from January loss)	7,500	Merchandise inventory, February 28	70,000
Income tax:		Office salaries expense	20,000
On continuing operations	10,000	Office supplies expense	935
Reduction applicable to loss		Purchases	251,200
from disposal of a segment		Rent expense	1,000
of the business	400	Sales	375,700
Reduction applicable to		Sales salaries expense	26,250
extraordinary loss	1,600	Store supplies expense	3,150

There was no change in the number of shares of common stock outstanding. Print the worksheet when done. *Check figure: February net income, $36,620.*

CHART (optional)

From the test data worksheet, develop a pie chart that presents the percentage distribution of selling expenses. Print the chart when done.

M11 ♦ BOOK VALUE PER SHARE

A prospective investor has hired you to develop a worksheet that will compute the book value per share (file name BVALUE) on each class of stock of various companies. Your worksheet should include a Data Section.

One of the companies the investor is currently interested in is McCain Enterprises, which has the following capital structure:

Preferred 14% stock, $35 par	$1,575,000
Premium on preferred stock	96,000
Common stock, $30 par	2,025,000
Premium on common stock	123,000
Retained earnings	525,000

Preferred stock has a prior claim to assets on liquidation to the extent of 120% of par.

Review the Model-Building Problem Checklist on page 173 to ensure that your worksheet is complete. Print the worksheet when done. *Check figure: Book value per share, McCain Enterprises: Common, $36.36.*

To test your model, use the following data for Robinson Corporation:

Preferred 12% stock, $45 par	$1,350,000
Premium on preferred stock	127,500
Common stock, $25 par	1,875,000
Premium on common stock	135,000
Retained earnings	487,500

Preferred stock has a prior claim to assets on liquidation to the extent of 110% of par.

Print the worksheet when done. *Check figure: Book value per share, Robinson Corporation: Common, $33.20.*

CHART (optional)

Using the test worksheet, prepare a pie chart that shows how much of the total equity is allocated to preferred stock and how much is allocated to common stock. Print the chart when done.

M12 ◆ DEFERRED INCOME TAX

Differences in accounting methods between those applied to its accounts and those used in determining taxable income yielded the following amounts for the first three years of Kibby Tool and Die:

	First Year	Second Year	Third Year
Income before income tax	$593,000	$614,000	$647,000
Taxable income	539,000	623,000	630,000

The income tax rate for each of the three years was 40% of taxable income, and taxes were paid promptly each year. The president of Kibby has asked you to develop a worksheet (file name DEFERTAX) that will show income tax deducted on the income statement, income tax payments for the year, year's addition to (deduction from) deferred income tax payable, and the year-end balance of deferred income tax payable. Use the information above as input for the Data Section of your worksheet.

Review the Model-Building Problem Checklist on page 173 to ensure that your worksheet is complete. Print the worksheet when done. *Check figure: Kibby Tool and Die, year-end balance of deferred tax payable, third year, $24,800.*

The president of Weatherwax Enterprises is impressed with your model and wishes to test it using the following data from Weatherwax (assume a 35% tax rate):

	First Year	Second Year	Third Year
Income before income tax	$657,000	$652,000	$664,000
Taxable income	627,000	660,000	675,000

Print the worksheet when done. *Check figure: Weatherwax Enterprises year-end balance of deferred tax payable, third year, $3,850.*

CHART (optional)

Using the Weatherwax Enterprises data, create a 3-D column chart showing the annual addition to or reduction in deferred taxes for all three years. Print the chart when done.

M13 ♦ BOND PREMIUM AND DISCOUNT AMORTIZATION SCHEDULE

On July 1, Horton Company issued $800,000 of 10-year, 14% bonds at an effective interest rate of 13%. This netted the company $843,410. Interest on the bonds is payable annually on July 1. The president of Horton has asked you to develop an amortization schedule worksheet (file name AMORT) that will use the effective interest method to calculate annual interest expense, premium (or discount) amortization, unamortized premium (or discount), and bond carrying amount. Your worksheet should include a Data Section.

Review the Model-Building Problem Checklist on page 173 to ensure that your worksheet is complete. Print the worksheet when done. *Check figure: Amortization of bond premium in year 10, $7,080.*

To test your model, calculate the annual interest expense, discount amortization, unamortized discount, and bond carrying amount of $600,000 of 10-year, 8% bonds at an effective interest rate of 9%. The issuance of these bonds netted the company $561,494. Interest on the bonds is payable annually. Print the worksheet when done. *Check figure: Amortization of bond discount in year 10, $5,505.*

CHART (optional)

With information from the test data, create a 3-D area chart that shows annual interest paid and interest expense over the 10-year life of the bond. Print the chart when done.

M14 ◆ CASH FLOW FROM OPERATING ACTIVITIES

Regina Company reported a net income of $52,500 for the current year. Depreciation recorded for the year totaled $19,000. Current asset and liability accounts had the following balances at the beginning and end of the year:

	Ending	Beginning
Cash	$41,300	$39,500
Accounts receivable	55,000	49,000
Inventory	69,800	70,300
Prepaid rent	5,400	5,200
Accounts payable	43,700	47,000
Notes payable	6,000	5,600

The president of Regina Company has asked you to develop a worksheet that will compute cash flow from operating activities (file name CASHFL). Use the information above as input for the Data Section of your worksheet.

Review the Model-Building Problem Checklist on page 173 to ensure that your worksheet is complete and ready to be graded. Print the worksheet when done. *Check figure: Cash flow from operating activities, $62,900.*

To test your model, use the information below for the following year, when net income was $30,000 and depreciation totaled $22,500.

	Ending	Beginning
Cash	$43,000	$41,300
Accounts receivable	51,200	55,000
Inventory	70,300	69,800
Prepaid rent	4,750	5,400
Accounts payable	40,500	43,700
Notes payable	5,000	6,000

Print the worksheet when done. *Check figure: Cash flow from operating activities, $52,250.*

CHART (optional)

Using the test model data, design a column chart that will show the components of cash flow from operating activities (net income, change in accounts receivable, etc.). Print the chart when done.

M15 ◆ VERTICAL ANALYSIS

Annette manages several rental properties for real estate investors. Each month she reviews the cash flow statements from each property to look for trouble spots. Information for one of the properties, Brown's Lake Apartments, is as follows:

Brown's Lake Apartments
Statement of Cash Receipts and Expenses

Revenue:		
Rental revenue		$750,000
Vending machine revenue		7,500
Total revenue		$757,500
Expenses:		
Advertising expense	$ 8,000	
Administrative expense	44,100	
Utilities expense	60,000	
Maintenance and repairs expense	54,500	
Real estate tax expense	88,200	
Insurance expense	6,000	
Interest expense	309,000	
Total expenses		569,800
Net cash flow		$187,700

Annette has asked you to develop a worksheet that will automatically prepare a vertical analysis of the cash flow data (file name VERT). All percentages should be based on total revenue. Use the data above as input for your model.

Review the Model-Building Problem Checklist on page 173 to ensure that your worksheet is complete. Print the worksheet when done. *Check figure: Interest expense is 41% of total revenue.*

To test your model, use the following information for Riverview Manor.

Riverview Manor
Statement of Cash Receipts and Expenses

Revenue:

Rental revenue		$135,000
Vending machine revenue		9,930
Total revenue		$144,930

Expenses:

Advertising expense	$ 3,330	
Administrative expense	5,075	
Utilities expense	8,475	
Maintenance and repairs expense	3,375	
Real estate tax expense	12,000	
Insurance expense	3,330	
Interest expense	$30,000	
Total expenses		65,585
Net cash flow		$ 79,345

Print the worksheet when done. *Check figure: Interest expense is 21% of total revenue.*

CHART (optional)

Using the test data worksheet, prepare a pie chart of the expenses. Use short titles for the X-axis. Print the chart when done.

M16 ♦ PROCESS COSTING: FIFO

Proven Industries uses FIFO process costing in accounting for its production activities. Materials are added at the beginning of the process and conversion costs are incurred uniformly throughout the process.

May's production records indicate the following information:

Quantities:
Beginning inventory (60% complete)	1,300 units
Started during May	2,800 units
Transferred to finished goods	3,100 units
Ending inventory (80% complete)	1,000 units

Beginning inventory costs:
Materials	$21,800
Direct labor	28,000
Factory overhead	14,000

May's production costs:
Materials	$46,000
Direct labor	81,000
Factory overhead	40,000

Design a cost of production report worksheet (file name FIFOPRC) for Proven that can be used by the company at the end of each month. Your worksheet should include a Data Section. Use the May data as input for your report.

Review the Model-Building Problem Checklist on page 173 to ensure that your worksheet is complete and ready to be graded. Print the worksheet when done. *Check figure: Total equivalent unit cost in May, $55.21.*

Using the following data for June, test your model:

Quantities:
Beginning inventory (80% complete)	1,000 units
Started during June	2,500 units
Transferred to finished goods	2,400 units
Ending inventory (30% complete)	1,100 units

Beginning inventory costs:
Materials	$16,429
Direct labor	20,769
Factory overhead	10,257

June's production costs:
Materials	$42,000
Direct labor	62,800
Factory overhead	30,000

Print the worksheet when done. *Check figure: Total equivalent unit cost in June, $64.88.*

CHART (optional)

Prepare a stacked-bar chart that shows the proportionate amount of materials, labor, and overhead each month that make up the cost of each completed unit. Print the chart when done.

M17 ♦ PROCESS COSTING: WEIGHTED AVERAGE

Ivana Industries uses weighted average process costing in accounting for its production activities. Materials are added at the beginning of the process and conversion costs are incurred uniformly throughout the process.

August's production records indicate the following information:

Quantities:	
Beginning inventory (60% complete)	1,300 units
Started during August	2,800 units
Transferred to finished goods	3,100 units
Ending inventory (80% complete)	1,000 units
Beginning inventory costs:	
Materials	$21,800
Direct labor	28,000
Factory overhead	14,000
August's production costs:	
Materials	$46,000
Direct labor	81,000
Factory overhead	40,000

Design a cost of production report template (file name WAPRC) for Ivana that can be used by the company at the end of each month. Your worksheet should include a Data Section. Use the August data as input for your report.

Review the Model-Building Problem Checklist on page 173 to ensure that your worksheet is complete and ready to be graded. Print the worksheet when done. *Check figure: Total equivalent unit cost in August, $58.33.*

Using the following data for September, test your model:

Quantities:	
Beginning inventory (80% complete)	1,000 units
Started during September	2,500 units
Transferred to finished goods	2,400 units
Ending inventory (30% complete)	1,100 units
Beginning inventory costs:	
Materials	$16,537
Direct labor	22,359
Factory overhead	11,077
September's production costs:	
Materials	$42,000
Direct labor	62,800
Factory overhead	30,000

Print the worksheet when done. *Check figure: Total equivalent unit cost in September, $62.97.*

CHART (optional)

Using the test model data, prepare a pie chart that shows the proportionate amount of materials, labor, and overhead that make up the cost of each completed unit. Print the chart when done.

M18 ♦ HIGH-LOW POINTS METHOD

An examination of monthly production and cost data over a period of several months for Industrial Edge reveals that the highest and lowest levels of production are as follows:

	Total Units Produced	Total Costs
Highest level	180,000	$423,000
Lowest level	75,000	255,000

It is estimated that 135,000 units will be produced next month. Develop a worksheet (file name HL) that can be used to calculate variable cost per unit and total fixed cost using the high-low points method. Then use the estimate to calculate the estimated cost of producing next month's output.

Review the Model-Building Problem Checklist on page 173 to ensure that your worksheet is complete. Print the worksheet when done. *Check figure: Estimated variable cost per unit for Industrial Edge, $1.60.*

To test your model, use the following information from Danforth Inc.:

	Total Units Produced	Total Costs
Highest level	3,300	$44,300
Lowest level	1,800	33,500

Estimate the cost of producing 3,200 units. Print the worksheet when done. *Check figure: Estimated variable cost per unit for Danforth Inc., $7.20.*

CHART (optional)

From the test data worksheet, create an XY chart plotting the high and low points. Use units produced as the X-axis (X-axis range) and total costs as the Y-axis (Series 1). Print the chart when done.

M19 ♦ COST-VOLUME-PROFIT ANALYSIS

In 2004, Sorrento Enterprises anticipates fixed costs of $300,000. Variable costs and expenses are expected to be 60% of sales. The president has asked you to develop a worksheet to calculate sales needed to break even and sales needed to achieve any desired net income (file name DESNI). Your worksheet should include a Data Section that contains fixed costs, desired net income, and variable costs as a percentage of sales. Assume as initial input for your model that the company wishes to achieve a net income of $75,000.

Review the Model-Building Problem Checklist on page 173 to ensure that your worksheet is complete. Print the worksheet when done. *Check figure: Sales needed for desired net income, $937,500.*

To test your model, use the following projections for 2005: fixed costs of $375,000 and variable costs and expenses to equal 40% of sales. The company wishes to have a net income of $90,000. Print the worksheet when done. *Check figure: Sales needed for desired net income, $775,000.*

CHART (optional)

Using the test data worksheet, develop a standard break-even line chart that plots total revenue and total costs from a sales level of $0 to $900,000. Use $100,000 increments on the X-axis.

M20 ♦ COST-VOLUME-PROFIT ANALYSIS (MULTIPLE PRODUCTS)

Data related to the expected sales of Resisto, Tam, and Yllem for Chamorro Industries for December are as follows:

Product	Selling Price Per Unit	Variable Cost Per Unit	Sales Mix
Resisto	$ 90	$ 70	50%
Tam	200	130	28%
Yllem	140	95	22%

Estimated fixed costs for December are $200,000, and Chamorro wants to realize an operating profit of $80,000.

Develop a worksheet (file name CVPMULTI) that will compute Chamorro's break-even point and the level of sales required to achieve its desired operating profit. The answers should be expressed both in units and in dollars, and they should be computed for the company as a whole and for the individual products, assuming they are sold in the proportions shown above.

Review the Model-Building Problem Checklist on page 173 to ensure that your worksheet is complete and ready to be graded. Print the worksheet when done. *Check figure: Break-even sales, $667,342.*

To test your model, change the following data for January: Resisto variable cost, $65; Tam selling price, $210; Resisto sales mix, 45%; and Yllem sales mix, 27%. *Check figure: Break-even sales, $598,690.*

CHART (optional)

Using the test model data, develop a pie chart that shows the sales mix proportion allocated to each product. Print the chart when done.

M21 ♦ JIT COST SAVINGS

Key Products is considering implementing a just-in-time program in its Muffler Fabrication Division. Several factors have been considered, and the following estimates have been made regarding possible savings and costs for the first year of the JIT implementation:

- Projected annual insurance costs of $80,000 will decline by 60% because of the lower average inventory.
- A leased 8,000 square foot warehouse, previously used for raw material storage, will not be needed. Key has obligated itself to pay the $11,200 lease this year, but has found tenants to sublet three-quarters of the building at $2.50 per square foot for the year. The remainder of the building will remain idle.
- Two warehouse employees whose services are no longer needed will be transferred to the Purchasing Department to assist in the coordination of the JIT program. The annual salary expense for these two employees totals $38,000 and will continue to be charged to the indirect labor portion of fixed overhead.
- Key anticipates using overtime to fabricate as many as 7,500 mufflers to meet emergency demands. The overtime premium will amount to $5.60 per muffler.
- In spite of using overtime to meet emergency demands, Key estimates it will lose 3,800 unit sales during the year due to stockouts.
- The Muffler Fabrication Division's average inventory will decline from $550,000 to $150,000.

Key Products Muffler Fabrication Division budgeted income statement for the next year, without any adjustment for the JIT program, is presented below. Key's borrowing rate related to inventory is 15 percent. All Key divisional budgets are prepared using an effective income tax rate of 40 percent.

Muffler Fabrication Division
Budgeted Income Statement

Sales (28,000 mufflers)		$ 616,000
Cost of goods sold		
Variable	$266,000	
Fixed	112,000	(378,000)
Gross profit		$ 238,000
Selling and administrative expense		
Variable	$ 70,000	
Fixed	55,500	(125,500)
Operating income		$ 112,500
Interest expense		(15,000)
Income before taxes		$ 97,500
Income taxes		(39,000)
Net income		$ 58,500

You have been asked to develop a worksheet (file name JIT) to assist in deciding whether to implement the JIT program. Use the data above as input for your worksheet.

Review the Model-Building Problem Checklist on page 173 to ensure that your worksheet is complete. Print the worksheet when done. *Check figure: After-tax savings, $25,800.*

To test your model, perform the following sensitivity analysis: the president of Key Products is comfortable with all of the projections except for lost sales, which she thinks can be higher than anticipated. Use the worksheet to determine how high lost sales can go before the benefit of the JIT program has disappeared. Print the worksheet when done. *Check figure: After-tax savings, $0.*

CHART (optional)

From the test data worksheet, design a 3-D column chart showing the total savings or cost associated with each of the factors listed. Print the chart when done.

(CMA, adapted)

M22 ♦ CASH BUDGETING

Puss & Pup Pet Store is concerned about its cash position at the end of November because of the anticipated inventory buildup during that month to get ready for the holiday season. Selected information about expected November activity is presented below:

Cash balance, November 1, 2004	$14,000
Sales	$210,000
Gross profit percent (based on sales)	45%
Decrease in accounts receivable during month	$12,000
Increase in accounts payable during month	$51,000
Increase in inventory during month	$90,000

Selling expenses total $32,000 per month plus 15% of sales. Depreciation expense of $5,000 per month is included in fixed selling expenses.

Prepare a worksheet (file name CASHBGT) that will allow Puss & Pup to compute its projected cash balance at the end of November. Your worksheet should include a Data Section and it should be designed so that it could be reused any month.

Review the Model-Building Problem Checklist on page 173 to ensure that your worksheet is complete. Print the worksheet when done. *Check figure: Projected ending cash balance, $23,000.*

To test your model, use the following estimates for December:

Cash balance, December 1, 2004	$23,000
Sales	$270,000
Gross profit percent (based on sales)	40%
Increase in accounts receivable during month	$30,000
Increase in accounts payable during month	$15,000
Decrease in inventory during month	$36,000

Selling expenses total $39,000 per month plus 14% of sales. Depreciation expense of $6,000 per month is included in fixed selling expenses. Print the worksheet when done. *Check figure: Projected ending cash balance, $81,200.*

CHART (optional)

Using the test worksheet, prepare a 3-D column chart showing the effects that sales, cost of goods sold, change in accounts receivable, change in accounts payable, and change in inventory have on the projected ending cash balance. Print the chart when done.

M23 ♦ DEVELOPING STANDARD COSTS

Nickerson Chemicals wishes to calculate the standard cost for a new liquid car wax it has developed called Shiner. The following information is available for the production of this product:

a. 60 gallons of the chemical Jase are heated to boiling. Jase is purchased in 55-gallon drums that cost $20 per drum.

b. Three gallons of the chemical Kase are added at this point and boiling continues for 30 minutes. Kase costs $1.81 per gallon.

c. During boiling, evaporation causes the loss of 12% of the mixture. The loss is normal, and its cost should be included in the cost of the wax produced.

d. After the mixture cools, 3 quarts of Lase are added and the chemical result is the product Shiner. Lase costs $2.44 per gallon.

e. Shiner is poured into 1-gallon plastic bottles and is packaged in cardboard cases holding 12 bottles. The plastic bottles cost $.17 each and the cardboard boxes cost $.48 each.

f. Direct production labor consists of 3 minutes per gallon of good output. Packaging labor is 7 minutes per case. The direct production labor rate is $11 per hour and the packaging labor rate is $8.16 per hour.

g. Variable overhead is 120 percent and fixed overhead 140 percent of total direct labor dollars.

Develop a standard cost worksheet for Nickerson (file name STANDARD) that itemizes the materials, labor, and overhead costs for one case of Shiner. Round the costs to the nearest penny. Hint: Compute the cost of one gallon or one batch first. This problem is tougher than it looks!

Review the Model-Building Problem Checklist on page 173 to ensure that your worksheet is complete. Print the worksheet when done. *Check figure: Cost of a case of Shiner, $36.00 (rounded).*

To test your model, assume that a supplier has informed Nickerson that the price of Jase is expected to rise to $20.37 per gallon and the price of Lase will increase to $2.95 per gallon. Also, due to new labor contracts, production labor will increase to $11.38 and packaging labor will increase to $8.20. Recompute the standard cost of a case of Shiner. Print the worksheet when done. *Check figure: New cost of a case of Shiner, $37.00 (rounded).*

CHART (optional)

Using the test model data, create a bar chart that discloses the cost of the various materials used in a case of Shiner. Print the chart when done.

M24 ♦ VARIANCE ANALYSIS

Hook Manufacturing makes dashboards for cars. During June, 40,000 dashboards were manufactured with standard costs and actual costs for direct materials, direct labor, and factory overhead as follows:

	Standard Costs	**Actual Costs**
Direct materials	10,000 pounds $9	10,600 pounds $10.50
Direct labor	20,000 hours $13	20,600 hours $12.50
Factory overhead	Rates per direct labor hour, based on normal capacity of 30,000 labor hours:	
	Variable cost $5.00	Variable cost $84,000
	Fixed cost $3.75	Fixed cost $49,000

You have been asked to develop a worksheet that will calculate the quantity variance, price variance, total direct materials cost variance, time variance, rate variance, total direct labor cost variance, volume variance, controllable variance, and total factory overhead cost variance (file name VARIANCE). Use the information above as input for the Data Section of your worksheet.

Review the Model-Building Problem Checklist on page 173 to ensure that your worksheet is complete. Print the worksheet when done. *Check figure: Factory overhead volume variance, $37,500 U.*

To test your model, use the following information for the manufacture of 60,000 dashboards during July:

	Standard Costs	**Actual Costs**
Direct materials	16,000 pounds $11	14,800 pounds $11.75
Direct labor	30,000 hours $15	28,400 hours $16.25
Factory overhead	Rates per direct labor hour, based on normal capacity of 30,000 labor hours:	
	Variable cost $5.00	Variable cost $133,000
	Fixed cost $3.75	Fixed cost $98,000

Print the worksheet when done. *Check figure: Factory overhead volume variance, $0.*

CHART (optional)

Using the test model worksheet, create a 3-D column chart that plots the four materials and labor variances (quantity, price, time, and rate). Print the chart when done.

M25 ♦ FLEXIBLE BUDGET FOR OVERHEAD

Needham Manufacturing prepares a flexible budget each month for its factory overhead expenses. The format for the budget is shown below. The budget amounts entered are for July.

Factory Expense Category	Budget Amount	Units of Production			
		16,000	17,000	18,000	19,000
Variable (per unit):					
Utilities	$ .75	$_____	$_____	$_____	$_____
Factory supplies	1.70	_____	_____	_____	_____
Repairs	.30	_____	_____	_____	_____
Fixed (in total):					
Rent	$5,000	_____	_____	_____	_____
Insurance	2,250	_____	_____	_____	_____
Total budgeted factory overhead		$_____	$_____	$_____	$_____

Prepare a worksheet (file name FLEX) that will calculate the amount that Needham should budget for each level of production. Design the worksheet so that it can be reused each month with new budget and/or unit data.

Review the Model-Building Problem Checklist on page 173 to ensure that your worksheet is complete and ready to be graded. Print the worksheet when done. *Check figure: total budgeted overhead at 16,000 units, $51,250.*

To test your model, use the following budget and unit data for August:

Units of production: 15,000, 17,000, 19,000, and 21,000

Utilities	$ .78	Rent	$5,250
Factory supplies	1.65	Insurance	$2,300
Repairs	.25		

Print the worksheet when done. *Check figure: Total budgeted overhead at 15,000 units, $47,750.*

CHART (optional)

Using the test model data, create an XY chart showing total factory overhead cost from 0 to 21,000 units of production. Print the chart when done.

M26 ◆ SEGMENT CONTRIBUTION TO INCOME

Selected data from the records of Shenna's Apparel for 2003 are as follows:

Net sales:	
Department R	$122,000
Department S	70,000
Department T	53,000
Cost of merchandise sold:	
Department R	$ 44,000
Department S	38,000
Department T	31,000
Direct expenses:	
Department R	$ 24,000
Department S	25,000
Department T	13,000
Indirect expenses	30,000
Income tax	10,000

Shenna has asked you to develop worksheet (file name SEGMARGIN) showing an income statement departmentalized through departmental margin.

Review the Model-Building Problem Checklist on page 173 to ensure that you worksheet is complete and ready to be graded. Print the worksheet when done. *Check figure: 2003 Net income, $30,000.*

To test your model, use the following information for 2004:

Net sales:	
Department R	$137,000
Department S	72,000
Department T	52,000
Cost of merchandise sold:	
Department R	$ 46,000
Department S	40,000
Department T	30,000
Direct expenses:	
Department R	$ 26,000
Department S	27,000
Department T	14,500
Indirect expenses	35,000
Income tax	11,500

Print the worksheet when done. *Check figure: 2004 Net income, $31,000.*

CHART (optional)

Using the test model data, create a column chart showing net sales, cost of merchandise sold, and direct expenses by department. Print the chart when done.

C1 ♦ FINANCIAL STATEMENT PREPARATION

Trail-Max Enterprises, a chain of stores servicing the eco-tourism industry, has provided you with the following list of accounts and balances for the year ended June 30, 2004. All amounts shown are in thousands of dollars. You have been asked by the company's chief financial officer (CFO) to use a spreadsheet to prepare financial statements for Trail-Max, including an income statement, a statement of retained earnings, a classified balance sheet, and (if required by your instructor) a statement of cash flows. The CFO can't remember the accounts receivable balance. She asks you to figure it out when you prepare the balance sheet.

The financial information presented below is accumulated in a file named FINANCL on your Student Disk. You are encouraged to use this file for preparing your statements and to use the information in this file as a Data Section for your answer. Place the statements in the space below the data. The financial statements should be shown in thousands of dollars just as in the Data Section. Trail-Max is a privately held company, so earnings per share information is not required.

	6/30/04	6/30/03
Accounts payable (for inventory purchases)	$ 382.4	$ 385.9
Accounts receivable	?	157.9
Accumulated depreciation—building	256.4	236.8
Accumulated depreciation—fixtures	344.8	364.5
Advances from customers	10.5	12.9
Advertising expense	135.5	128.0
Allowance for bad debts	6.3	6.3
Bad debt expense	11.5	15.0
Bonds payable (due 9/1/09)	458.3	258.3
Buildings	583.2	583.2
Cash	56.4	49.4
Common stock	235.2	211.2
Copyrights	10.4	11.2
Cost of goods sold	2,863.9	3,244.0
Depreciation expense	113.9	102.0
Discontinued operations loss (net of tax)	188.3	-0-
Dividends declared on common	100.9	90.0
Dividends declared on preferred	10.6	10.6
Fixtures	894.7	868.5
Gain on sale of old fixtures	54.4	-0-
Goodwill	53.4	56.7
Income tax expense	140.1	20.0
Income tax payable	37.5	50.0
Interest expense	38.8	35.0
Interest payable	7.1	4.7
Inventories	345.1	255.1
Land	100.9	100.9
Long-term notes payable	49.7	60.8

Other operating expenses	345.6	500.0
Paid-in capital in excess of par	180.7	166.7
Preferred stock	132.9	132.9
Prepaid advertising	32.8	42.1
Rent expense	-0-	325.0
Retained earnings (beginning of year)	306.5	269.1
Salaries expense	623.1	714.0
Salaries payable	60.6	55.7
Sales	4,586.6	5,383.0
Short-term investments	133.9	28.0
Short-term notes payable	4.7	13.9
Supplies expense	128.2	162.0
Treasury stock (at cost)	114.1	114.1

Additional information required for the statement of cash flows:

- Trail-Max sold a large amount of obsolete and worn out fixtures for $64.4. The fixtures originally cost $124.0 and had been depreciated down to a net book value of $10.0.
- Additional common stock was issued in July. Twelve thousand shares of common stock were issued in July for $38,000. The par value of the stock is $2 per share.
- Write off of goodwill and amortization copyrights are included in other operating expenses.
- No bonds were retired during the year. No additional notes payable were issued during the year.
- Short-term investments of $110.0 were made during the year. Trail-Max also sold $4.1 short-term investments at no gain or loss.

Review the Model-Building Problem Checklist on page 173 to ensure that your model is complete. Use the Print Preview command (File menu) to make sure that the worksheet will print neatly, then print the worksheet. *Check figure: Total assets, $1,692.6.*

To test your model, suppose the auditors made the following three adjustments to the June 30, 2004 balances: sales were reduced by $50,000 to 4,536.6; inventories were increased by $30,000 to 375.1; and accounts payable were increased by $80,000 to 462.4. Record these adjustments to your model. Does your balance sheet still balance? Print the worksheet again. *Check figure: Total assets, $1,722.6.*

CHART (optional)

Using the test data worksheet, create a pie chart showing all major sources of funding for Trail-Max at year-end: current liabilities, long-term liabilities, and stockholders' equity. Print the chart when done.

	A	B	C	D	E	F	G
2	**FINANCL**						
3	*Financial Statement Preparation*						
4							
5	Trail-Max Enterprises						
6							
7						6/30/04	6/30/03
8	Accounts payable					$382.4	$385.9
9	Accounts receivable					???	157.9
10	Accumulated depreciation - buildings					256.4	236.8
11	Accumulated depreciation - fixtures					344.8	364.5
12	Advances from customers					10.5	12.9
13	Advertising expense					135.5	128.0
14	Allowance for bad debts					6.3	6.3
15	Bad debt expense					11.5	15.0
16	Bonds payable (due 9/1/09)					458.3	258.3
17	Buildings					583.2	583.2
18	Cash					56.4	49.4
19	Common stock					235.2	211.2
20	Copyrights					10.4	11.2
21	Cost of goods sold					2,863.9	3,244.0
22	Depreciation expense					113.9	102.0
23	Discontinued operations loss (net of tax)					188.3	0.0
24	Dividends declared on common					100.9	90.0
25	Dividends declared on preferred					10.6	10.6
26	Fixtures					894.7	868.5
27	Gain on the sale of old fixtures					54.4	0.0
28	Goodwill					53.4	56.7
29	Income tax expense					140.1	20.0
30	Income tax payable					37.5	50.0
31	Interest expense					38.8	35.0
32	Interest payable					7.1	4.7
33	Inventories					345.1	255.1
34	Land					100.9	100.9
35	Long-term notes payable					49.7	60.8
36	Other operating expenses					345.6	500.0
37	Paid in capital in excess of par					180.7	166.7
38	Preferred stock					132.9	132.9
39	Prepaid advertising					32.8	42.1
40	Rent expense					0.0	325.0
41	Retained earnings (beginning of year)					306.5	269.1
42	Salaries expense					623.1	714.0
43	Salaries payable					60.6	55.7
44	Sales					4,586.6	5,383.0
45	Short-term investments					133.9	28.0
46	Short-term notes payable					4.7	13.9
47	Supplies expense					128.2	162.0
48	Treasury stock (at cost)					114.1	114.1
49							

C2 ◆ FINANCIAL ANALYSIS

The following financial information has been abstracted from the 2005 annual report of Zach's Incorporated. Zach's is a traditional department store retailer operating 82 stores under 12 different names. They cater to middle to upper-middle income customers and are widely known for service and value. They offer a wide selection of quality merchandise with special emphasis placed on fashion apparel, accessories, and fashion home furnishings. You have been asked by the company's president and chief operating officer (COO) to use a spreadsheet program to analyze the data and prepare a report for him giving your assessment of Zach's current financial position.

The financial information presented below is accumulated in a file named ANALYSIS on your Student Disk. You are encouraged to use this file for preparing your analysis and to use the information in this file as a Data Section for your answer.

Five-Year Selected Financial Data	2005	2004	2003	2002	2001
Operating Results			(in millions)		
Net sales	$ 2,367	$ 2,313	$ 2,266	$ 2,156	$ 2,028
Cost of goods sold	1,671	1,595	1,551	1,476	1,378
Selling, general & admin. exp.	527	502	480	452	432
Provision for relocation		10			
Interest expense	23	23	23	23	24
Interest income	(4)	(4)	(3)	(3)	(3)
Other income	(29)	(26)	(22)	(19)	(18)
Income before income taxes	179	213	237	227	216
Income taxes	55	83	93	98	105
Net income	124	130	144	130	111
Financial Position					
Cash	$ 45	$ 71	$ 87	$ 97	$ 106
Receivables	667	644	625	589	548
Inventories	393	393	362	332	307
Other current assets	12	5	2	2	2
Total current assets	1,117	1,113	1,076	1,020	963
Net property and equipment	445	408	355	310	295
Investments and other assets	35	27	21	23	21
Total assets	1,597	1,548	1,452	1,353	1,279
Total current liabilities	$ 182	$ 240	$ 244	$ 246	$ 275
Long-term debt	241	231	227	235	236
Retained earnings	1,163	1,066	969	861	756
Stockholders' equity	1,174	1,077	981	872	768

Other Data

Capital expenditures for property and equipment	$ 82	$ 97	$ 92	$ 58	$ 64
Depreciation	35	36	37	38	34
Dividends declared and paid	27	34	35	26	21
Number of shares outstanding	37	37	37	37	37
Year-end stock market price*	45	50	93	70	56
Number of stores at year-end*	82	80	80	79	82
Total square feet (thousands)*	12,683	12,077	11,791	11,124	11,105

*not in millions

Quarterly Data

2005	1st Q	2nd Q	3rd Q	4th Q	Total
Sales	$494	$515	$571	$787	$2,367
Income before taxes	42	25	50	62	179
Net income	28	17	34	45	124

2004	1st Q	2nd Q	3rd Q	4th Q	Total
Sales	$478	$505	$555	$775	$2,313
Income before taxes	44	27	56	86	213
Net income	27	16	34	53	130

Industry Statistics

Current ratio, 3.5
Quick ratio, 2.0
Accounts receivable turnover, 8.38
Days' sales in receivables, 44
Inventory turnover, 3.65
Days' sales in inventory, 100
Times-interest earned, 5.2
Asset turnover, 1.66
Return on total assets, 7.67%
Return on equity, 12.09%
Price-earnings ratio, 18
Dividend yield, 2.5%
Dividend payout ratio, 31%
Gross profit (margin) ratio, 38.1%
Profit margin, 2.94%
Long-term debt to equity ratio, .55
Overall debt ratio, 47%

Common size income statement

Sales	100%
Gross profit	38
Income before taxes	7
Net income	3

Common size balance sheet

Cash	6%
Accounts receivable	30
Inventory	27
Property and equipment	37
Current liabilities	18%
Long-term debt	29
Stockholders' equity	53

Monthly sales as a percent of total sales

	Sales
January	5.3%
February	5.8
March	7.4
April	7.4
May	7.8
June	7.4
July	6.7
August	8.1
September	8.0
October	8.2
November	10.7
December	17.2
	100.0%

Selected five-year industry statistics:

	2005	2004	2003	2002	2001
Sales per square foot	$248	$193	$219	$206	$178
Sales growth (year-to-year)	9.3%	8.7%	9.3%	8.3%	6.0%

Check off the ratios below that your instructor wants you to include in your report. You will want to group these ratios by type according to your textbook (profitability, liquidity, and so forth). Compute them for all five years. Some ratios require average balances rather than year-end figures. Since figures are not available for 2000, use year-end balances rather than average amounts for 2001 ratios. Zach's has no preferred stock. Your instructor may also provide you with additional ratios or statistics to compute. Enter them at the bottom of each list.

In your analysis, note Zach's current position as well as important trends. Describe changes in profitability, liquidity, long-term solvency, and so forth. Evaluate these changes in light of the future. Compare ratios to industry standards.

Standard Ratios and Statistics

a. Working capital

b. Current ratio

c. Acid test (quick) ratio

d. Accounts receivable turnover

e. Number of days' sales in receivables

f. Inventory turnover

g. Number of days' sales in inventory

h. Times-interest-earned

i. Total asset turnover

j. Rate of return on total assets

k. Rate of return on stockholders' equity

l. Earnings per share

m. Dividends per share

n. Price-earnings ratio

o. Dividend yield

p. Dividend payout ratio

q. Gross profit (margin) ratio

r. Profit margin (net income/sales)

s. Long-term debt to equity ratio

t. Overall debt ratio

u. Book value per share

v.

w.

x.

Trends

a. Sales

b. Cost of goods sold

c. Gross profit

d. Selling, general and administrative expenses

e. Income before taxes

f. Net income

g.

Other

a. Sales per square foot

b. Common size income statements (vertical analysis)

c. Common size balance sheets (vertical analysis)

d. Statement of cash flows for 2002–2005

e. Comparative income statements between years 2005 and 2004 (horizontal analysis—compute dollar change and percent change)

f. Comparative balance sheets between years 2005 and 2004 (horizontal analysis—compute dollar change and percent change)

g.   Seasonal sales and income analysis (only two years available)

h.

Review the Model-Building Problem Checklist on page 173 to ensure that your model is complete and ready to be graded. Use the Print Preview command (File menu) to make sure that the worksheet will print neatly, then print the worksheet. *No check figures are provided.*

No test data is provided for this model.

CHART (optional)

Prepare a 3-D area chart comparing earnings per share and dividends per share over the five-year period. Print the chart when done.

	A	B	C	D	E	F
2		*ANALYSIS*				
3		*Financial Analysis*				
4						
5		Zach's Inc.				
6						
7	Yearly Data					
8						
9	Operating Results	2005	2004	2003	2002	2001
10	Net sales	$2,367	$2,313	$2,266	$2,156	$2,028
11	Cost of goods sold	1,671	1,595	1,551	1,476	1,378
12	Selling, general & admin. exp.	527	502	480	452	432
13	Provision for relocation		10			
14	Interest expense	23	23	23	23	24
15	Interest income	(4)	(4)	(3)	(3)	(3)
16	Other income	(29)	(26)	(22)	(19)	(18)
17	Income before income taxes	179	213	237	227	216
18	Income taxes	55	83	93	98	105
19	Net Income	124	130	144	130	111
20						
21	Financial Position	2005	2004	2003	2002	2001
22	Cash	$45	$71	$87	$97	$106
23	Receivables	667	644	625	589	548
24	Inventories	393	393	362	332	307
25	Other current assets	12	5	2	2	2
26	Total current assets	1,117	1,113	1,076	1,020	963
27	Net property and equipment	445	408	355	310	295
28	Investments and other assets	35	27	21	23	21
29	Total assets	1,597	1,548	1,452	1,353	1,279
30						
31	Total current liabilities	$182	$240	$244	$246	$275
32	Long-term debt	241	231	227	235	236
33	Retained earnings	1,163	1,066	969	861	756
34	Stockholders' equity	1,174	1,077	981	872	768
35						
36	Other Data	2005	2004	2003	2002	2001
37	Capital expenditures for property & equip.	$82	$97	$92	$58	$64
38	Depreciation	35	36	37	38	34
39	Dividends declared and paid	27	34	35	26	21
40	Number of shares outstanding	37	37	37	37	37
41	Year-end stock market price	$45	$50	$93	$70	$56
42	Number of stores at year end	82	80	80	79	82
43	Total square feet	12,683	12,077	11,791	11,124	11,105
44						
45	Quarterly Data					
46						
47	2005	1st Q	2nd Q	3rd Q	4th Q	Total
48	Sales	$494	$515	$571	$787	$2,367
49	Income before taxes	42	25	50	62	179
50	Net income	28	17	34	45	124
51						
52	2004	1st Q	2nd Q	3rd Q	4th Q	Total
53	Sales	$478	$505	$555	$775	$2,313
54	Income before taxes	44	27	56	86	213
55	Net income	27	16	34	53	130

C3 ♦ THREE-MONTH MASTER BUDGET

The balance sheet of Big Bud Corp. as of June 30, 2004 is as follows:

Big Bud Corp.
Balance Sheet
June 30, 2004

Assets

Cash		$ 20,850
Accounts receivable		96,000
Raw materials		51,120
Finished goods		32,200
Land		25,000
Plant and equipment	$250,000	
Less: Accumulated depreciation	56,000	194,000
		$419,170

Liabilities and Stockholders' Equity

Accounts payable to suppliers		$ 20,000
Common stock	$ 50,000	
Retained earnings	349,170	399,170
		$419,170

The following information has been extracted from Big Bud's records:

1. Big Bud manufactures and sells Noiblas. The company has projected unit sales for its product for the next five months as follows:

	Units
July	7,000
August	8,000
September	10,000
October	8,000
November	7,000

All sales are made on account. Noiblas sell for $30 each. Forty percent of all sales are collected in the month of sale. The remaining 60% are collected in the following month.

2. Management desires to maintain the finished goods inventory for Noiblas at 20% of the following month's sales. Big Bud's June 30, 2004 finished goods inventory consists of 1,400 Noiblas.

3. In order to produce one Noibla, the following units of raw materials are used:

Raw Material	Units
BPP	5
Winkle	3

    The price of BPP has recently risen and is now $2 per unit. The price of Winkle is $1.40 per unit. Management desires to maintain the ending raw materials inventory for both BPP and Winkle at 25% of the following month's production needs. Big Bud's June 30, 2004 raw material inventory consists of 18,000 units of BPP (@ $2.00 each) and 10,800 units of Winkle (@ $1.40 each).

4. Seventy percent of all purchases are paid in the month of purchase. The remaining 30% are paid in the subsequent month.

5. The company's product requires 30 minutes of direct labor time to complete. All labor costs are paid in the month incurred. Each hour of direct labor costs $12.

6. Factory overhead is applied at the rate of $6 per direct labor hour. Actual overhead costs are paid as they are incurred. Monthly differences between applied and actual overhead costs are expected to be negligible.

7. Selling and administrative expenses are $5,000 per month plus 10% of sales. They are paid in the month incurred.

8. Plant and equipment depreciates at the rate of $6,000 per year. This depreciation is incurred evenly throughout the year and is included in the factory overhead costs mentioned above.

Design a worksheet (file name BIGBUD) for Big Bud Corp. to prepare the following July, August, and September budgets for 2004: sales budget, production budget, raw materials purchases budget, cash budget, projected unit cost to produce one Noibla, budgeted income statement, and budgeted balance sheet. Use a column of the worksheet for each month and a final column for totals for the quarter. Round budget calculations (except unit costs) to the nearest dollar. The sales budget and raw materials purchases budgets should be expressed both in units and dollars. Big Bud uses FIFO cost flow assumption for valuing inventories.

The acid test for developing this model: When you are done, are your balance sheets in balance?

Review the Model-Building Problem Checklist on page 173 to ensure that your worksheet is complete and ready to be graded. Use the Print Preview command (File menu) to make sure that the worksheet will print neatly, then print the worksheet. *Check figure: Total assets at the end of September, $518,429.*

To test your model, increase the price of Noibla to $35 and change August sales units to 9,000. Does your worksheet calculate throughout, and do your balance sheets balance?

Print the worksheet again. *Check figure: Total assets at the end of September, $639,229.*

CHART (optional)

Using the test data, create a 3-D area chart that compares monthly cash flow (change in the cash account) with monthly net income. Print the chart when done.

	A	B	C	D	E
2	**BIGBUD**				
3	*Three-Month Master Budget*				
4					
5	Big Bud Corp.				
6	Balance Sheet, June 30, 2004				
7					
8	Cash			$20,850	
9	Accounts receivable			96,000	
10	Raw materials			51,120	
11	Finished goods			32,200	
12	Land			25,000	
13	Plant and equipment		$250,000		
14	Less: accumulated depreciation		56,000	194,000	
15	Total assets			$419,170	
16					
17	Accounts payable to suppliers			$20,000	
18	Common stock		$50,000		
19	Retained earnings		349,170	399,170	
20	Total liabilities and equity			$419,170	
21					
22					
23	Budgeted Noibla sales in units				
24	July		7,000		
25	August		8,000		
26	September		10,000		
27	October		8,000		
28	November		7,000		
29	Selling price		$30		
30	Collections from customers				
31	Collected in month of sale		40%		
32	Collected the following month		60%		
33	Desired finished goods inventory				
34	(% of next month's unit sales)		20%		
35	Desired raw material inventory				
36	(% of next month's production needs)		25%		
37	Raw material units needed to produce one Noibla				
38	BPP		5		
39	Winkle		3		
40	Beginning inventory units & cost				
41	Noibla		1,400	$23.00	
42	BPP		18,000	$2.00	
43	Winkle		10,800	$1.40	
44	Purchases				
45	Paid in the month of purchase		70%		
46	Paid in the subsequent month		30%		
47					
48	Direct labor time to produce one Noibla		0.5 hours		
49	Cost of direct labor		$12 per hour		
50	Factory overhead		$6 per direct labor hr.		
51					
52	Selling and administrative expenses		$5,000 fixed		
53			10% variable		
54	Plant and equipment depreciation		$6,000 per year		